To Donna
From Marcella,
Your Sister In Christ

JOHN

3/09

Chapters 1—10

D1009815

J. Vernon McGee

THOMAS NELSON PUBLISHERS

Nashville • Atlanta • London • Vancouver

Published in Nashville, Tennessee, by Thomas Nelson, Inc.

Scripture quotations are from the KING JAMES VERSION of the Bible.

Library of Congress Cataloging-in-Publication Data

McGee, J. Vernon (John Vernon), 1904–1988
    [Thru the Bible with J. Vernon McGee]
    Thru the Bible commentary series / J. Vernon McGee.
        p.   cm.
    Reprint. Originally published: Thru the Bible with J. Vernon McGee. 1975.
    Includes bibliographical references.
    ISBN 0-7852-1041-5 (TR)
    ISBN 0-7852-1101-2 (NRM)
    1. Bible—Commentaries.   I. Title.
BS491.2.M37   1991
220.7′7—dc20
                                                                90–41340
                                                                CIP

PRINTED IN MEXICO
20 – 10 09 08 07

this is not a polemic Gospel at all and he is not attempting to meet that issue. Also, there are those who say that it is a supplement to what the others had written, that he merely added other material. But Hase answers that by saying, "This Gospel is no mere patchwork to fill up a vacant space."

You see, these theories do not give an adequate answer to account for all the peculiar facts that are in this Gospel which a true explanation must do. And, in my judgment, the only satisfactory explanation is that John wrote at the request of the church which already had three Gospels (Matthew, Mark, and Luke were being circulated) and wanted something more spiritual and deep, something that would enable them to grow. That's exactly what Augustine, the great saint of the early church, said:

> In the four Gospels, or rather in the four books of the one Gospel, the Apostle St. John not undeservedly with reference to his spiritual understanding compared to an eagle, has lifted higher, and far more sublimely than the other three, his proclamation, and in lifting it up he has wished our hearts also to be lifted (Gregory, *Key to the Gospels,* pp. 285–286).

That is the purpose of the Gospel of John. That is the reason that he wrote it.

Accordingly, therefore, when we come to the Gospel of John, we find that he does not take us to Bethlehem. We will never grow spiritually by singing "O Little Town of Bethlehem" umpteen times at Christmas. John won't take us to Bethlehem because he wants you and me to grow as believers. John takes us down the silent corridors of eternity, through the vast emptiness of space, to a beginning that is not a beginning at all. "In the beginning was the Word" (John 1:1). Some say that this world came into being three billion years ago. I think they're pikers. I think it has been around a lot longer than that. What do you think God has been doing in eternity past, twiddling His thumbs? May I say to you, He had a great deal to do in the past, and He has eternity behind Him. So when you read, "In the beginning," go as far back as your little mind can go into eternity past, put down your peg—and Jesus Christ comes out of eternity to meet you. "In the beginning was [not is] the Word, and the Word was with God, and the Word was God" (John 1:1). Then come on down many more billions of years. "All things were made by him; and without him was not any thing made that was made" (John 1:3). Then John, in the fourteenth verse, takes another step: "And the Word was made flesh, and dwelt among us" (John 1:14).

The Greek philosophers and the Greek mind for which Luke wrote would stop right there and say, "We're through with you. We can't follow you." But John was not writing for them, and he goes even further. "No man hath seen God at any time; the only begotten Son, which is in the bosom of the Father, he hath declared him" (John 1:18). "Declared him" is *exegeted* Him, led Him out in the open where man can see Him and come to know Him. The Man who had no origin is the Son who comes out of eternity.

Luke, who was a medical doctor, looked at Him under a "microscope." Though John's method is altogether different, he comes to the same conclusion as did Luke. You could never call John's method scientific. The Christian who has come to a knowledge of Christ and faith in Him doesn't need to have the virgin birth gone over again; he already believes that. Therefore, when he comes to the Gospel of John, he finds sheer delight and joy unspeakable as he reads and studies it.

Unfortunately, though, he thinks the unbeliever ought to have it also. And you'll find it is used in personal work more than any other Gospel. After all, doesn't the average Christian consider it the simple Gospel? Is it simple? It's profound. It's for believers. It enables them to grow.

When I was a pastor in Pasadena, I had a doctor friend who, because of his position, was able to get together students at Cal Tech for a Bible class. Do you know what he taught? You're right, the Gospel of John. He told me, "You know, I really shook that bunch of boys with the first chapter." I met him several weeks after that and asked him how the class was getting on. "Oh," he said, "they quit coming." Well, after all, they had been in a school where you pour things into a test tube, where you look at things under a microscope. I said, "Why didn't you take the Gospel of Luke?" "Because," he said, "I wanted to give them the simple Gospel." Well, he didn't. John is not simple; it's profound. It is for believers.

Also there was a seminary professor in this area not long ago who was asked to teach the Bible to a group of businessmen at a noon luncheon. Guess what book he taught. You're right! He said, "They don't know very much, so I'll give them the Gospel of John." I wish he'd given them the Gospel of Mark. That's the Gospel of action, the Gospel of power, the Gospel for the strong man. But he gave them the Gospel of John.

The Gospel of John is for those who already believe. When you come to chapters thirteen through seventeen you can write a sign over it, *For Believers Only,* and you could put under that, *All Others Stay Out.* I don't think that section was ever meant for an unbeliever. Jesus took His own into the Upper Room and revealed to them things that enabled them to grow. And no other Gospel writer gives us that. Why? Because they're the evangelists who are presenting Christ as the Savior of the world. Somebody asks, "But doesn't John do that?" Yes, he does, but he is primarily writing for the growth of believers.

John gives more about the resurrected Christ than does any other Gospel writer; in fact, more than all the others put together. Paul said that, though we have known Christ after the flesh, we don't know Him that way anymore. Rather, we know Him as the resurrected Christ. For this reason John attempts to give the appearances of Jesus after His resurrection, and he mentions seven of them.

The first was one of the most dramatic as He appeared to Mary Magdalene there in the garden. The second was to the disciples in the Upper Room, Thomas being absent. The third appearance was again to the disciples in the Upper Room with Thomas present (these three appearances are recorded in ch. 20). Then we see Him appearing by the Sea of Galilee. Several disciples were out fishing. He called to them from the shore, "Do you have any fish?" (see John 21:5).

He is going to ask you that some day, and He's going to ask me. Have you been doing any fishing recently? Well, you catch them only the way He tells you. You have to fish by His instructions.

And then He prepared breakfast for them. I wish I had been there for that outdoor breakfast. That was a real cookout. And, friend, He still wants to feed you in the morning—also during the day and in the evening—with spiritual food. Then He commissioned Simon Peter: "Simon, do you love Me?" (see John 21:15–17). Jesus did not say that you have to be a graduate of a seminary to be able to serve Him. He asked, "Do you love Me?" That's the one condition. Don't misunderstand me. If you love Him, you will want training to prepare you for the ministry He has for you, but He wants to know that you love Him. The reason multitudes of folk are not serving Him today is that they do not love Him. And then Peter was told that he was to be a martyr; but John, no, he will live on in order to write this Gospel, three epistles, and the Book of Revelation. There are the seven appearances that John records, and all of them are for believers; they minister to us today.

At the time of the birth of Christ there was a great expectation throughout the heathen world. That was a strange thing.

> Suetonius relates that "an ancient and definite expectation had spread throughout the East, that a ruler of the world would, at about that time, arise in Judaea." Tacitus makes a similar statement. Schlegel mentions that Buddhist missionaries traveling to China met Chinese sages going to seek the Messiah about 33 A.D. (*Life of Vespasian*, c. iv.).

There was an expectation throughout the world at that time that He might come. And it was out of the mysterious East that the wise men came to Jerusalem, "Saying, Where is he that is born King of the Jews? . . ." (Matt. 2:2).

The marvel is that this Gospel of John, so definitely designed to meet the need of believers, is also designed for the oriental mind as is no other. Whom do I mean by Orientals? The Egyptians, the Babylonians, the Persians, the uncounted millions in India and in China. Even to this good day we know so little about that area of the world. What about Tibet or Outer Mongolia? It is still the mysterious East. We do know this: there is fabulous wealth there, and right next to it is abject poverty. Out of this land of mystery came the wise men. They were bringing gifts—gold, frankincense, and myrrh for Him. There are a lot of questions to be answered there. Out of that land of mystery they came. That Oriental splendor that we've heard so much about reveals unbelievable wealth, and it is still there—ornate palaces, gaudy grandeur, priceless gems. It has so entranced the West that, when Columbus started out for this country (we give him credit for discovering America, but he wasn't looking for our continent), he was trying to find a new route to the East in order to bring back something of the wealth that was there.

However, by the side of that wealth there is extreme poverty of the basest sort, dire destitution, millions living in squalor and misery. Their worldly goods consist of the rags they have on their backs. One hundred million will die of starvation in this next decade, we're told. You may ask, "Well, why don't we send food for them?" There's not enough to go around. Our decision is what hundred million will starve? Will it be these or those? But the thing that arrests us is that the poor were crying for help, and the wealthy had found no solution to the problems of life. The Orient gave freest reign to human desires. Although they had this freedom, there was no satisfaction. They've had the great pagan religions—Buddhism, Shintoism, Hinduism, Confucianism, and Mohammedanism. Yet out of that area, with all that they had, their wise men came asking, ". . . Where is he that is born King of the Jews? for we have seen his star in the east, and are come to worship him" (Matt. 2:2). They needed salvation. They had none; no religion ever gave that to them. And this is the reason people in the mysterious East have reveled in the Gospel of John as no others have. It is a mind today that will revel in the Gospel of John. The Lord Jesus can meet the need of this type of mind, as John reveals.

Out of heaven's glory He came, that One who was before any beginning that we can envision. "And the Word was made flesh" and walked down here among men. The Orient had religion. After all, Israel belonged to that area of the world. The Orient had all kinds of religion. They had temples—ornate, hideous, with degrading rituals. They had cults of the occult. And John tells us that the first public act of the Lord Jesus was to go into the temple of that day and cleanse it. By this He is telling them something, these people who worshiped in their degrading temples, that God is *holy*. If you're going to worship

God you'll have to be cleansed; the temple will have to be cleansed; there can be no compromise with evil or wrong.

A religious ruler came to Jesus one night—John alone tells us this. Our Lord that night said to this religious ruler, who had everything and was religious to his fingertips, "You must be born again" (see John 3:3). He needed to have a new life and get rid of the old religion. Jesus said that He had not come to sew a patch on the old garment, but He came to give them the robe of righteousness that would enable them to stand before a holy God. This is what that area of the world needed.

Womanhood was degraded in the Orient. Our Lord ennobled womanhood because He came, born of a woman. He went to a wedding to answer the mockery that they'd made of marriage with the harems of the East. Christ went to a wedding and put His blessing upon it. Also Jesus sat down at a well and had a conversation with a woman of very questionable character. But she was a woman for whom He later died. The soul of a woman was as precious to Him as the soul of a man.

Christ fed the multitudes, followed the meal with a discourse on the Bread of Life, and then escaped because He did not want them to make Him king of their stomachs.

The oriental mind would understand Jesus' discourse on the Bread of Life. It is unfortunate that the managers of our supermarkets don't understand it—they think it's bread and beans on the shelf that's important, and He said it's not. A man in the Orient who hasn't bread and beans will understand that. I am afraid some of us miss it today.

The Lord Jesus said in this Gospel, "I am the light of the world; I am the bread of life; I am the way, the truth and the life." And the Orient was wretched and perishing in that day, as it is today. John says, "And many other signs truly did Jesus in the presence of his disciples, which are not written in this book: but these are written, that ye might believe that Jesus is the Christ, the Son of God; and that believing ye might have life through his name" (John 20:30–31). The thing that they needed above everything else was life. And, friend, this is what the whole world needs today—not religion, but life!

Now before we begin our study of this magnificent Gospel, let me call your attention to some striking features.

The first three Gospels are called the synoptic Gospels because they are written from the same viewpoint with a similar pattern. The fourth Gospel is different.

1. Matthew and Mark emphasize the miracles of Jesus, and Luke gives attention to the parables. John does neither.

2. The miracles in John are given as signs and were chosen with a great deal of discrimination in order to interpret certain great truths. (For example, the discourse on the Bread of Life follows the feeding of the five thousand.) There are eleven specific signs in the Gospel of John.

3. There are no parables in the fourth Gospel. The word *parable* does occur one time in John 10:6, but it is not the regular Greek word *parabolē* but *paroimia*. This word ought not to be translated "parable" at all. The story of the Good Shepherd is not a parable; it is a discourse.

John gives us a chronological order which is well to note. The fact of the matter is, if you will follow it along, it will give you a ladder on which you can fit the three-year ministry of Christ. (For example, in John 1:29, 35 he says, "The next day . . . , the next day.") He's giving not only a logical but also a chronological sequence in his Gospel. He also gives attention to places and cities—for example, "Bethabara beyond Jordan" (John 1:28); "Cana of Galilee" (John 2:1).

The deity of Christ is emphasized in this Gospel and is actually in the foreground. But the humanity of Christ is not lost sight of. Do you notice it is only John who tells about His trip through Samaria, and that He sat down at the well, and that He was weary with His journey? Can you think of anything more human than that? Well, I can think of one thing—Jesus wept. And it is John who tells us that, by the way.

The name *Jesus* is used almost entirely to the exclusion of *Christ* in this Gospel. That is strange because the emphasis is upon the deity of Christ, and you'd think that he would use the name *Christ*. Then why does he use the name *Jesus*? It is because God became a man.

There is a mighty movement in this Gospel, and it is stated in John 16:28. "I came forth from the Father, and am come into the world: again, I leave the world, and go to the Father." God became a man; this is the simple statement of the sublime fact.

OUTLINE

Another division of the Gospel of John:
LIGHT—John 1—12
LOVE—John 13—17
LIFE—John 18—21

CHAPTER 1

THEME: *Prologue—Incarnation; Word is God, Word became flesh, Word revealed God; witness of John the Baptist; witness of Andrew; witness of Philip; witness of Nathanael*

WORD IS GOD—WORD BECAME FLESH—WORD REVEALED GOD

In the beginning was the Word, and the Word was with God, and the Word was God [John 1:1].

The Gospel of John introduces the Lord Jesus Christ with three tremendous statements:

> "In the beginning was the Word,"
> "And the Word was with God,"
> "And the Word was God."

"The Word" is one of the highest and most profound titles of the Lord Jesus Christ. To determine the exact meaning is not easy. Obviously the Lord Jesus Christ is not the *logos* of Greek philosophy; rather He is the *memra* of the Hebrew Scriptures. Notice how important the Word is in the Old Testament. For instance, the name for Jehovah was never pronounced. It was such a holy word that they never used it at all. But this is the One who is the Word and, gathering up everything that was said of Him in the Old Testament, He is now presented as the One "In the beginning." This beginning antedates the very first words in the Bible, "In the beginning God created the heaven and the earth." That beginning can be dated, although I do not believe that anyone can date it accurately—it is nonsense to say that it is 4004 B.C., as Ussher's dating has it. It probably goes back billions and billions of years. You see, you and I are dealing with the God of eternity. When you go back to creation, He is already there, and that is exactly the way this is used—"in the beginning *was* the Word." Notice it is not *is* the Word; it was not in the beginning that the Word started out or was begotten. *Was* (as Dr. Lenske points out) is known as a durative imperfect, meaning continued action. It means that the Word was in the beginning. What beginning? Just as far back as you want to go. The Bible says, "In the beginning God created the heaven and the earth" (Gen. 1:1). Does that begin God? No, just keep on going back billions and trillions and "squillions" of years. I can think back to billions of years back of creation—maybe you can go beyond that—but let's put down a point there, billions of years back of creation. He already was; He comes out of eternity to meet us. He did not begin. "In the beginning *was* the Word"—He was already there when the beginning was. "Well," somebody says, "there has to be a beginning somewhere." All right, wherever you begin, He is there to meet you, He is already past tense. "In the beginning was the Word"—five words in the original language, and there is not a man on topside of this earth who can put a date on it or understand it or fathom it. This first tremendous statement starts us off in space, you see.

The second statement is this, "and the Word was with God." This makes it abundantly clear that He is separate and distinct from God the Father. You cannot identify Him as God the Father because He is *with* God. "But," someone says, "if He is with God, He is not God." The third statement sets us straight, "and the Word was God." This is a clear, emphatic declaration that the Lord Jesus Christ is God. In fact, the Greek is more specific than this, because in the Greek language the important word is placed at the beginning of the sentence and it reads, "God was the Word." That is emphatic; you cannot get it more emphatic than that. Do you want to get rid of the deity of Christ? My friend, you cannot get rid of it. The first three statements in John's Gospel tie the thing down. "In the beginning was the Word, and the Word was with God, and the Word was God."

Let's move on down to verse 14 and notice the three statements there.

And the Word was made flesh, and dwelt among us, (and we beheld his glory, the glory as of the only begotten of the Father,) full of grace and truth [John 1:14].

"And the Word was made flesh,"
"And the Word dwelt among us,"
"He was full of grace and truth."

The Greek philosopher probably would have stayed with us through verse one, but he leaves us here. He would never agree that the Word was made flesh. The Greek language allows us to put it more specifically and, I think, more accurately: "The Word was *born* flesh." Turn this over in your mind for a moment. Here comes God out of eternity, already the Ancient of Days; but He also came to Bethlehem, a little baby thing that made a woman cry. And notice that John's Gospel does not even mention His birth in Bethlehem. Do you know why? He is talking about One who is too big for Bethlehem. Out of eternity, the Word became flesh.

"And [the Word] dwelt among us" is the second statement in verse 14. "Dwelt" is from *skenoo;* it means "He pitched His tent among us." Our human bodies are merely little tents in which we live. The apostle Paul used the same imagery: ". . . we know that if . . . this tabernacle were dissolved . . ." (2 Cor. 5:1). This house in which we live is a tabernacle, a tent, that can be blown over in a night; it can be snuffed out in an instant. Because you and I live in these little tents, the God of eternity took upon Himself a human body and thus pitched His tent down here among us. Such is the second tremendous statement.

Notice the third, "(and we beheld his glory, the glory as of the only begotten of the Father,) full of grace and truth." Now John is saying something else. The question I would naturally ask at this point is, "If He was made flesh, He certainly limited himself." John says, "Wait a minute—He was full of grace and truth." The word "full" means that you just could not have any more. He brought all the deity with Him, and He was full of grace and full of truth when He came down here.

Now we move to verse 18 to find three statements again.

No man hath seen God at any time; the only begotten Son, which is in the bosom of the Father, he hath declared him [John 1:18].

> "No man hath seen God at any time;"
> "The only begotten Son, which
>   is in the bosom of the Father,"
> "He hath declared him."

Notice the first: "No man hath seen God at any time." Why? He will explain it in this Gospel; the Lord Jesus will tell the woman at the well, "God is a Spirit: and they that worship him must worship him in spirit and in truth" (John 4:24)—for God is spirit. No man has seen God at any time. What about the appearances in the Old Testament? God never revealed Himself in the Old Testament to the eyes of man. What, then, did they see? Well, go back and read the record. For instance, Jacob said that he saw God, but what he saw was the angel of the Lord who wrestled with him. That was a manifestation, but he did not see God because God is a spirit. "No man hath seen God at any time."

The second statement is, "the only begotten Son." The best Greek text is that of Nestle, the German scholar. He has come to the definite conclusion that it is not the only begotten Son, but the only begotten God. I prefer that also. "Which is in the bosom of the Father" tells us a great deal. He did not come from the head of God to reveal the wisdom of God; He did not come from the foot of God to be a servant of man. (Have you ever noticed that although we speak of the fact He was a servant, whose shoes did He ever shine? Did He ever run an errand for anybody? He did not. He said, "For I came down from heaven, not to do mine own will, but the will of him that sent me" [John 6:38]. He was God's servant—He came to serve Him, and as He served the Father, He served men.) He did not come from the feet; He did not come from the head; it was from the bosom of the Father that He came. He came to reveal the heart of God: He was "the only begotten Son, which is in the bosom of the Father."

The third statement completes verse eighteen: "he hath declared him." The Greek word here is *exegesato. Ago* is "to lead" and *ex* is "out." It means that what Jesus Christ did was to lead God out into the open. Do you know anything bigger than that? A little trip to the moon is nothing in comparison. Here He comes out of eternity past, the God of this universe, the Creator of everything, taking upon Himself human flesh, and bringing God out into the open so that men can know Him. My friend, the only way in the world you can know God is through this One, Jesus Christ. Jesus Christ came to reveal God because He is God.

I am not through with these statements; there is something else here. Let's put together the first verse in each of these three groups and see what we come up with:

> "In the beginning was the Word,"
> "And the Word was made flesh,"
> "No man hath seen God at any time."

You could not see God—God is spirit. He had to become flesh; He had to become one of us in order for us to know Him. We could not go up there to understand Him; He had to come down here and bring God down where we are.

Now let's put the second statements together from each of the three groups:

> "The Word was with God,"
> "And dwelt among us,"
> "The only begotten Son, which
>   is in the bosom of the Father."

Consider this One for a moment—the angels bowed before Him, He was with God, on an equality with God. The apostle Paul wrote of Him, He ". . . thought it not robbery to be equal with God" (Phil. 2:6). That is, He did not go to school to become God; it was not something He worked overtime to attain. It was not a degree that He earned. He did not *try* to be God; He *was* God. I do not mean to be irreverent, but He did not say to the Father when He came to this earth, "Keep your eye on Gabriel; he is after My job; watch him while I'm gone." He did not have to do that—nobody could take His place. He was God. Here

He comes: born in Bethlehem, a few little shepherds there, not many; He goes up to Nazareth, thirty years hidden away in Nazareth. God, out of eternity coming down and going to Nazareth, working in a carpenter shop. Why? So you can know God. The only way you will ever know Him, my friend, is to know this One. "The only begotten Son, which is in the bosom of the Father" is the only One who can reveal God to us.

Now notice the third statement in each group:

> "The Word was God,"
> "And we beheld his glory, the glory as of the only
>   begotten of the Father, full of grace and truth,"
> "He hath declared him."

When He was down here, He was still God, full of grace and truth. And He declared Him; He is the only one who can lead Him out in the open where we can get acquainted with Him.

We are not through with this. I want you to see something else. How do you divide up this universe? I sat with a man who designed the shield that has been on all these space crafts to make their re-entry. He is a scientist who is an authority on heat. As we had lunch together in New Jersey, he said, "You know, this universe is made up of just three things. I believe that God has put His fingerprints on everything—the Trinity is everywhere." Then he explained what he meant. The universe is divided up into time, space, and matter. Can you think of a fourth? The very interesting thing is that time, space, and matter include everything that is in this universe as you and I know it. Then time can be divided into just three parts: past, present, and future. Can you think of a fourth? And what about space? Length, breadth, and height. Is there another direction? Also there is in matter energy, motion, and phenomena. Those are the three divisions of the three divisions. The universe in which we live bears the mark of the Trinity.

Now notice the way in which the Incarnation is geared into this observation. Verse 1:

Time: "In the beginning was the Word, and the Word was with God."

Space: "The Word was made flesh"—became flesh, came down into space. Where? To Bethlehem, a little geographical spot—and even this earth was a pretty small spot for Him to come to—and He pitched His tent here among us. We beheld His glory, full of grace and truth.

Matter: "No man hath seen God at any time; the only begotten Son, which is in the bosom of the Father, he hath declared him." Because He became matter, became a man, took upon Himself humanity, men could see and know God. This is the time, space, and matter of the Incarnation. Let's divide each of these into three.

Past: "In the beginning *was* the Word."

Present: "The Word was made [became] flesh" (in our day).

Future: "No man hath seen God at any time; the only begotten Son . . . hath declared him." The apostle Paul, at the end of his life, said, "That I may know him, and the power of his resurrection . . ." (Phil. 3:10). That will be for the future—to really know Him; today we actually know so little because we are finite.

Then look at space, divided into length, breadth and height.

Length: "In the beginning was the Word."

Breadth: He came down to this earth and was made flesh.

Height: No man has seen God at any time; the only begotten Son, who is in the bosom of the Father—He has come from the heights to set Him before us.

Consider the divisions of matter: energy, motion, and phenomena.

Energy: In the beginning was the *Word*, and the *Word* was with God—that's energy. How did this universe come into existence? God spoke. Every rational person has to confront this problem of how this universe began. That is the reason evolution has been popular—it offers to the natural man an explanation for the origin of the universe. You must have an explanation for it if you do any thinking at all. Where did it come from? Well, here is the answer: "In the beginning was the Word." God spoke. That is the first thing that happened. When God speaks, when the Word speaks, energy is translated into matter. What is atomic fission? It is matter translated back into energy—poof! it disappears. Creation began with energy. In the beginning was the *Word*. The *Word* was with God. The *Word* was God.

Motion: The Word was made flesh. He came out of heaven's glory and He came to this earth.

Phenomena: The greatest phenomenon in this world is Jesus Christ. The wonders of the ancient world, the wonders to see in our day are nothing in comparison to the wonder of the Incarnation—God became man!

These statements are bigger than any of us, and yet they are so simple. We have read them, probably memorized them, yet no man can plumb the depths of them. "In the beginning was the Word, and the Word was with God, and the Word was God. . . . And the Word was made flesh, and dwelt among us, (and we beheld his glory, the glory as of the only begotten of the Father,) full of grace and truth. . . . No man hath seen God at any time; the only begotten Son, which is in the bosom of the Father, he hath declared him" (vv. 1, 14, 18).

These three verses are the great building blocks; now let us consider some of the cement that holds them together.

And things were made by him; and without him was not any thing made that was made [John 1:3].

The Lord Jesus Christ is the Creator. Not only did He exist before Bethlehem, but He created the vast universe including the material out of which man constructed Bethlehem. All things were made by Him; He is the instrument of creation. Nothing came into existence without Him.

In him was life; and the life was the light of men [John 1:4].

Now we are confronted with something else—two of the simplest things in the world: light and life. *Zoe* and *phos* are the two words in the original language. From *zoe* we get zoology, the study of life; and from *phos* we get photo or anything that is built on it, such as photograph—it is light. These two things are so common that we take them for granted. Life—we see it everywhere. There may be a great deal of life right where you are at this moment. You go out in the woods and you see the same thing—life. It greets you on every hand, but can you explain it? You see in the Sunday pictorials and the sensational magazines that men now have discovered the source of life. But if you read them, you find that they have not found the source at all, though they think they are close to it. They put the microscope down on a green leaf. One moment they see that a little cell is arranged one way and is dead as a doornail. The next moment the thing is rearranged in another way, and it is alive. And then the thing starts growing and doubling, dividing and multiplying itself. Why does it do that? Life.

The other common thing is light. What is light? I listened to Irwin Moon try to explain it (and Irwin gave the best explanation I have heard), but when he got through, I was not sure if light is a real something or if it is just waves because they can cut the thing off and still light will go through. As you know, certain kinds of light will go through objects that would stop waves. What in the world is light?

You see, we are dealing with things that are fundamental, though men today with all their scientific gadgets know so little about them.

"In him was life"—all life is in Jesus Christ. "In him was life; and the life was the light of men." You and I live in a universe that is spiritually dark. The fact of the matter is, it is physically dark to a certain degree. But God said, ". . . Let there be light . . ." (Gen. 1:3) and these light holders are placed about throughout His universe like street lights in a big city. We are told that when a man gets away from this earth a short distance, he is in total, absolute darkness, and it is frightening to be out where there is nothing from which the sun can be reflected. Our little globe is out in a dark universe, yet that is nothing compared to the spiritual darkness that envelops it. When the sun disappears, there is physical darkness over the land; but twenty-four hours a day there is spiritual darkness here, awful spiritual darkness. Man does not know God; man is in rebellion against God; man is in sin that blinds him to God. In the Lord Jesus Christ there is life, and the life that He gives is the *light* of men. In fact, His life is the only thing that can kindle light in the heart of an individual. An unregenerate man has no spiritual life within him. This is the reason that when you present to him Jesus Christ, he says, "I don't get it. I don't understand that at all."

I used to go down to the jail in Cleburne, Texas, and speak to the men. It was not a large jail and I could talk to them in a conversational tone. I would start off talking about football (because in Texas football is a religion!), and those hardened men would get enthusiastic about it. I talked also of other things and they were interested. Then I would turn the conversation to something spiritual, and I could see the darkness come over their faces. I might just as well have been talking to corpses. And that is what they were—men dead in trespasses and sins. This world today is in spiritual darkness, and the Lord Jesus Christ has brought the only light there is in the world. He is the light. "In him was life; and the life was the light of men."

And the light shineth in darkness; and the darkness comprehended it not [John 1:5].

That word "comprehend" is an unfortunate translation. And a wiseacre did not help it by rendering it, "and the darkness was not able to put it out." That is no translation at all. The word in the Greek is *katelaben,* meaning actually "to take down." It is the picture of a secretary to whom the boss is giving dictation, and she stops and says, "I can't take that down. I am not able to take it down." The light shines in darkness and the darkness is not able to take it in. That is it exactly. Someone said to him, "Boy, was I in darkness before I received Christ! And I don't know why I didn't see." Well, that is it: you were in darkness and you did not see. The darkness just cannot take it in.

Now this is something quite interesting, and it is not true of physical light. You go into a dark room, and the minute you switch on the light, the darkness leaves, it disappears. Darkness and light cannot exist together physically. The moment you bring light in, darkness is gone. The minute light is taken out, darkness will come right back in. But *spiritual* light and darkness exist together. Sometimes there is a husband who is saved and a wife who is unsaved—or vice versa. Here is a believer working next to another man who says, "What do you mean when you talk about being a Christian? I do the best I can. Am I not a Christian?" There you have light and darkness side by side and the darkness just cannot take it in. That is exactly what is said here, "The light shineth in darkness; and the darkness comprehended it not."

He was in the world, and the world was made by him, and the world knew him not [John 1:10].

That was the tragedy—the world was in darkness, spiritual darkness, and did not know Him. Even today we are seeing the rise of atheism and unbelief, and we will see it more and more in the days that lie ahead. A great many people do not seem to recognize that unbelief and atheism go naturally with the natural man. Somebody says to me, "Oh, did you read in the paper what Dr. So-and-So of a certain seminary wrote?" Yes, I read it. "Well, isn't it awful?" No, I do not think so. He would upset my apple cart if he said that he believed the Bible because he is an unbeliever by his own statement. He says that he does not believe in being born again, that he does not believe he has to receive Christ in order to be saved. Now I do not expect that man to say he believes the Bible. That would be absolutely contrary to his statements. The so-called theologians and theological professors who espouse the "God is dead movement" present us with the preposterous, untenable claim that they are Christian atheists! Obviously atheism precludes the possibility of being Christian, yet unbelief has moved into our seminaries and pulpits across the land. The world does not know Him.

He came unto his own [his own things], and his own [people] received him not [John 1:11].

He came into His own universe but His own people did not receive Him.

But as many as received him, to them gave he power to become the sons of God, even to them that believe on his name [John 1:12].

"But as many as received him, to them gave he power." The word *power* is not *dunamis* power like dynamite, physical power, but *exousian* power which is delegated power, authority. "But as many as received him, to them gave he the *authority* to become the sons of God [children, *tekna* of God], even to them that believe on his name."

Notice that this is for "them that *believe* on his name." And always with the word "believe" there is a preposition. You see, faith, as the Bible uses it, is not just head knowledge. Many people ask, "You mean all that I have to do is to say I believe?" Yes, that is all you have to do, but let's see what that implies. With the verb "to believe" there is always a preposition—sometimes *en* (in), sometimes *eis* (into), or sometimes *epi* (upon). You must believe into, in, or upon Jesus Christ. Let me illustrate with a chair. I am standing beside a chair and I believe it will hold me up, but it is not holding me up. Why? Because I have only a head knowledge. I just say, "Yes, it will hold me up." Now suppose I believe into the chair by sitting in it. See what I mean? I am committing my entire weight to it and it is holding me up. Is Christ holding you up? Is He your Savior? It is not a question of standing to the side and saying, "Oh, yes, I believe Jesus is the Son of God." The question is have you trusted Him, have you believed into Him, are you resting in Him? This chair is holding me up completely. And at this moment Christ is my complete Savior. I am depending on Him; I am resting in Him.

WITNESS OF JOHN THE BAPTIST

And this is the record of John, when the Jews sent priests and Levites from Jerusalem to ask him, Who art thou? [John 1:19].

This is the first incident in the life of John the Baptist which John gives us in his Gospel record. He does not give us the story of the beginning of this man. We find out about his birth in the Gospel of Luke, but here the record of John the Baptist begins when a delegation from Jerusalem comes to question him. They come out to ask him, "Who art thou?"

In this question there is a subtle temptation because this offered

John an opportunity to make something of himself. In John 3:30 we find his response when his disciples wanted him to make something of himself. He said, "He must increase, but I must decrease." What a statement that is! That is a statement that every believer should make. But every believer should live it too. "He must increase, but I must decrease." Friend, both can't be on top. Either Christ is primary in your life and occupies first place, or you (that is, the selfish "I") will be on top. You can't have both. He must increase and I must decrease, or else it will be the other way around.

Now note the answer that he gives to the religious rulers:

And he confessed, and denied not; but confessed, I am not the Christ [John 1:20].

You see, they cleverly suggest that he might be the Messiah—they have a messianic hope. But he makes it very clear that he is not the Christ; he is not the Messiah. They are looking to the wrong man. So, if he is not the Christ, what great person is he?

And they asked him, What then? Art thou Elias? And he saith, I am not. Art thou that prophet? And he answered, No [John 1:21].

You notice how brief and matter-of-fact John is here. His answers are terse, and they get briefer as the religious rulers continue to question him. If he's not the Christ, he must be Elijah. If he's not Elijah, he must be "that prophet." They are referring to a prophet "like unto Moses" who had been promised back in Deuteronomy 18:15. John gives an emphatic "No!" He is not the predicted prophet of Deuteronomy.

Then said they unto him, Who art thou? that we may give an answer to them that sent us. What sayest thou of thyself? [John 1:22].

They insist that he must tell them who he is. They can't take back a report of just a string of negatives. So John does identify himself.

He said, I am the voice of one crying in the wilderness, Make straight the way of the Lord, as said the prophet Esaias [John 1:23].

Notice that he is a voice. You see, Christ is the Word! John is the voice! A voice is all John wants to be. He has a grand message to give, a message much greater than he is. Frankly, we should be satisfied to be only a voice because certainly the message we have to give is greater than the individual. And that voice should, of course, declare the glories of Christ.

Notice the grand message that he gives, "Make straight the way of the Lord." In other words, "Get ready for the coming of the Lord." I take it that he means the Kingdom of Heaven is at hand. It was at hand in the person of the King, you see. And he tells them to "Make straight the way." This would be the same as telling them to get the crooked things out of their lives, to deal with the things that are wrong. This we need to do also. When we do that, there is opened for us fellowship with God. "If we say that we have fellowship with him, and walk in darkness, we lie, and do not the truth" (1 John 1:6). We need to get our lives straight, and we can get them straight by confession, as we are taught in 1 John 1:8–9.

You will notice that he says he is quoting the prophet Isaiah. ". . . Prepare ye the way of the Lord, make straight in the desert a highway for our God" (Isa. 40:3).

And they which were sent were of the Pharisees.

And they asked him, and said unto him, Why baptizest thou then, if thou be not that Christ, nor Elias, neither that prophet? [John 1:24–25].

They are now presenting him with a technical point. "If you are none of these, then why do you baptize?"

John answered them, saying, I baptize with water: but there standeth one among you, whom ye know not;

He it is, who coming after me is preferred before me, whose shoe's latchet I am not worthy to unloose [John 1:26–27].

Today, we call this man John the Baptist. But he said that he merely used water. There was One coming after him who would baptize with fire and with the Holy Spirit. That fire is the baptism of judgment which is to come upon the earth. The baptism of the Holy Spirit took place at Pentecost. One wonders whether Christ was in the crowd that day. We don't know. But He might have been.

"He . . . coming after me is preferred before me, whose shoe's latchet I am not worthy to unloose." A servant must do every task of his master. A disciple, however, must do every task except take the thong out of the teacher's shoes. That was the rule of that day. John is saying that he is a servant. He is not even a disciple; he is merely a servant. And he is not even worthy to be that servant, although that is what he is.

These things were done in Bethabara beyond Jordan, where John was baptizing [John 1:28].

I called attention in the Introduction to the fact that the apostle John gears us into the geography and to the calendar. Here we have a geographical location given to us. And then notice that the following verse begins, "The next day." John is showing to us that the One who came from out of eternity, the Word made flesh, is now geared into geography and into our calendar down here.

The next day John seeth Jesus coming unto him, and saith, Behold the Lamb of God, which taketh away the sin of the world [John 1:29].

John marks Him out here. He is the Savior. He is not only the Messiah; He is also the Savior. He is a very great Savior for He is the Lamb of God. He is the complete Savior because He takes away sin. He is the almighty Savior because He takes away the sin of the world. He is the perpetual Savior because He "taketh" away—present tense. Anyone can come to Him at any time.

Here we find the fulfillment of the answer that Abraham had given to Isaac those many years ago. Isaac had said, ". . . Behold the fire and the wood: but where is the lamb for a burnt offering? And Abraham said, My son, God will provide himself a lamb for a burnt offering . . ." (Gen. 22:7–8). John tells us that Jesus is the Lamb.

This proves that Cain was wrong and Abel was right. Abel brought a little lamb. All the lambs that were slain on Jewish altars down through the ages now find their fulfillment in Him. John marks Him out. "Behold the Lamb of God, which taketh away the sin of the world."

> **This is he of whom I said, After me cometh a man which is preferred before me: for he was before me.**
>
> **And I knew him not: but that he should be made manifest to Israel, therefore am I come baptizing with water [John 1:30–31].**

John is saying that Jesus is the real Baptizer. We might call Him Jesus the Baptizer. He is the One who will baptize with the Holy Spirit and with fire.

> **And John bare record, saying, I saw the Spirit descending from heaven like a dove, and it abode upon him.**
>
> **And I knew him not: but he that sent me to baptize with water, the same said unto me, Upon whom thou shalt see the Spirit descending, and remaining on him, the same is he which baptizeth with the Holy Ghost.**
>
> **And I saw, and bare record that this is the Son of God.**
>
> **Again the next day after John stood, and two of his disciples;**
>
> **And looking upon Jesus as he walked, he saith, Behold the Lamb of God! [John 1:32–36].**

Before it was the Lamb of God that taketh away the sin of the world. That is the *work* of Christ. Now it is "Behold the Lamb of God!" He is the Lamb in His *person*. We see that John baptized Jesus and that Jesus was identified by the Holy Spirit. So, looking upon Jesus as He walked, John says, "Behold the Lamb of God!"

WITNESS OF ANDREW

And the two disciples heard him speak, and they followed Jesus.

Then Jesus turned, and saw them following, and saith unto them, What seek ye? They said unto him, Rabbi, (which is to say, being interpreted, Master,) where dwellest thou?

He saith unto them, Come and see. They came and saw where he dwelt, and abode with him that day: for it was about the tenth hour [John 1:37–39].

He extends the same invitation to you today, "Come and see." Taste of the Lord and see whether or not He is good (see Ps. 34:8).

Notice again how specifically John gears this into time—it was late in the evening.

One of these two who had been disciples of John the Baptist was Andrew, and the very first thing that he does is to go after his own brother, Simon.

One of the two which heard John speak, and followed him, was Andrew, Simon Peter's brother.

He first findeth his own brother Simon, and saith unto him, We have found the Messias, which is, being interpreted, the Christ.

And he brought him to Jesus. And when Jesus beheld him, he said, Thou art Simon the son of Jona: thou shalt be called Cephas, which is by interpretation, A stone [John 1:40–42].

This man, Simon, was as weak as water. Our Lord told him that he would be a stone man. I think everybody laughed there that day because nobody believed he could become the rock man, the man who would stand up on the Day of Pentecost and give the first sermon, which would be used to sweep three thousand persons into the church (see Acts 2:40–41).

WITNESS OF PHILIP

The day following Jesus would go forth into Galilee, and findeth Philip, and saith unto him, Follow me.

Now Philip was of Bethsaida, the city of Andrew and Peter [John 1:43–44].

Again we are dealing with geography. Bethsaida is up on the Sea of Galilee. We know that Peter and Andrew and Philip lived up there. They were fishermen.

Philip findeth Nathanael, and saith unto him, We have found him, of whom Moses in the law, and the prophets, did write, Jesus of Nazareth, the son of Joseph.

And Nathanael said unto him, Can there any good thing come out of Nazareth? Philip saith unto him, Come and see [John 1:45–46].

WITNESS OF NATHANAEL

This Nathanael is a wiseacre, and he makes a wisecrack here. Can any good thing come out of Nazareth? And I think he laughed at his own joke, by the way. But Philip didn't laugh. He just said, "Come and see." That is the really important thing—come and see.

Jesus saw Nathanael coming to him, and saith of him, Behold an Israelite indeed, in whom is no guile! [John 1:47].

Here is an Israelite in whom there is no Jacob. You see, although this man is a wisecracker, he is not deceitful or cunning. There is nothing of the old Jacob in him. He is an Israelite in whom there is no Jacob.

> **Nathanael saith unto him, Whence knowest thou me? Jesus answered and said unto him, Before that Philip called thee, when thou wast under the fig tree, I saw thee.**
>
> **Nathanael answered and saith unto him, Rabbi, thou art the Son of God; thou art the King of Israel [John 1:48–49].**

The Lord Jesus had two doubters among His apostles. The one at the beginning was Nathanael; the one at the end was Thomas. This man, this skeptic, this one who wonders whether any good can come out of Nazareth, confesses before the interview is over that Jesus is the Son of God, the King of Israel.

When Nathanael confessed that the Lord Jesus is the Son of God and the King of Israel, it reveals that something very important did come out of Nazareth.

> **Jesus answered and said unto him, Because I said unto thee, I saw thee under the fig tree, believest thou? thou shalt see greater things than these [John 1:50].**

The Lord more or less rebuked him and asked whether it was just because He saw him under the fig tree that he believed. Jesus promises him that he will see greater things. Indeed during the next three years, Nathanael did see much greater things than these.

> **And he saith unto him, Verily, verily, I say unto you, Hereafter ye shall see heaven open, and the angels of God ascending and descending upon the Son of man [John 1:51].**

Our Lord had said to this man, "Behold, an Israelite in whom there is no Jacob." Now He follows up on this by referring to the incident in the life of the patriarch Jacob when, as a young man, he had run away from home. In fact, he had to leave home because his brother Esau was after him to murder him. His first night away from home was at Bethel, and there the Lord appeared to him. A ladder was let down from heaven, and on that ladder the angels were ascending and descending. The meaning for Jacob was that God had not lost contact with him. He had thought that when he left home, he had left God back there. He had a limited view of God, of course. At Bethel he learned that God would be with him.

Our Lord picks that up here and says that the ladder was Himself. You'll see now the angels of God ascending and descending upon the Son of Man. The angels ministered to Him, and the angels were subject to Him. Here He was given charge over the angels. He could send them as messengers to heaven, and they would return also. So Jesus says that Nathanael will see heaven opened and the angels of God ascending and descending upon the Son of Man. He is going to see that the Father from the top of that ladder will speak of this One, saying, ". . . This is my beloved Son, in whom I am well pleased" (Matt. 3:17).

The ladder is Christ, and only by Him can you and I make contact with God. The Lord Jesus said, ". . . I am the way, the truth, and the life: no man cometh unto the Father, but by me" (John 14:6). He is the ladder—not one that you climb, but One that you trust, One that you rest upon and believe in. That is the important thing to see here.

This first chapter of John's Gospel has been lengthy and extremely important. The prologue presents the incarnation of the Word—He is God, He became flesh, He reveals the Father. Then He is introduced by witnesses. John the Baptist testifies that Jesus is the revealer of God. Andrew testifies that Jesus is the Messiah. Philip testifies that Jesus fulfills the Old Testament. Nathanael witnesses that Jesus is the Son of God, the King of Israel.

CHAPTER 2

THEME: Jesus at marriage in Cana (first work); Jesus cleanses temple during Passover in Jerusalem (first word); Jesus interviews Nicodemus in Jerusalem (second word)

JESUS AT MARRIAGE IN CANA (First Work)

The important incident in this chapter is when Jesus, invited to the marriage in Cana, performed His first miracle. We are told in the eleventh verse, "This beginning of miracles did Jesus." This, then, is the answer to those who teach that the Lord Jesus, as a little boy down in Egypt making clay pigeons with the other little boys, would touch the clay pigeons and they would fly away. That makes a pretty good story, but there is no fact in it. This record makes it very clear that He did not perform miracles in Egypt, but that His first miracle was at Cana of Galilee.

The wonder of all this is that here is the One who is in the beginning with God and is God. He came out of eternity. He was made flesh and for his first thirty years lived in Nazareth of Galilee. Then He walks over a hill to attend a wedding in Cana.

Notice that again John gears this in with time and space. "And the third day." Our Lord is now going out into His ministry.

> **And the third day there was a marriage in Cana of Galilee; and the mother of Jesus was there:**
>
> **And both Jesus was called, and his disciples, to the marriage [John 2:1–2].**

Many Bible teachers believe that she was there because she was related to the individuals who were getting married, or at least to one of the families. This is largely a supposition, but it could well be true. The Lord Jesus and His disciples were also invited.

The time is given here as the third day. It is thought that this was

probably late February or early March in the year A.D. 27. The very
interesting thing is that John carefully gives the places. In the pre-
vious chapter we were back in Bethsaida, and now the scene shifts to
Cana of Galilee. Then it will move to Capernaum in verse 12 and to
Jerusalem in verse 13. John gives us the chronological sequence and
the geography.

It says that "the mother of Jesus" was there. She is never called
Mary in the Gospel of John. She comes to Jesus with a very unusual
request. Notice what she says to Him.

**And when they wanted wine, the mother of Jesus saith
unto him, They have no wine [John 2:3].**

The question comes up about the wine. I read recently of a liberal who
called Jesus a bootlegger. Such sacrilege! In that day, wine was a sta-
ple article of diet. However, drunkenness was absolutely condemned.
There was no thought of drunkenness connected with this. A wedding was a religious occasion, by the way, and these were folk who
believed the Old Testament. You can put it down that there was no
intoxication at this wedding.

The wedding is a picture of another wedding that is coming.
Christ began His ministry on this earth at a wedding. He will conclude it, as far as the church is concerned, with a wedding. At the
marriage supper of the Lamb the church will be presented to Him as a
bride.

This is the first miracle which He performed. Moses' first miracle
was turning water into blood. Christ's first miracle was turning water
into wine. The Law was given by Moses, but grace and truth came by
Jesus Christ. What a contrast!

What did Mary mean by her statement? First of all, it is well to call
attention to the fact that this was a very poor family. They simply
didn't have enough refreshments. Bengal in his commentary said
that, when she told the Lord there was no wine, it was a gentle hint for
Him and His disciples to depart. Calvin writes that it was a suggestion
for Him to occupy the minds of the guests with a discourse. It would
be just like John Calvin to suggest that, by the way. If you have ever

read Calvin's *Institutes,* you know they are profound, but boring. If Calvin had been there, he would have given them a discourse and probably put them all to sleep! However, I do not think that the context here would permit either interpretation. I don't believe it was a hint for Him to leave nor a suggestion to occupy the minds of the guests. I think that very candidly she is saying, "Perform a miracle. This would be an appropriate occasion."

You will recall that when the angel Gabriel appeared to her and told her that she was the one who was to bring forth the Messiah, Mary raised the question about the virgin birth, ". . . How shall this be, seeing I know not a man?" (Luke 1:34). Gabriel made it very clear that the Holy Spirit would come upon her and that which was conceived in her was holy. She showed her faith and submission when she said, ". . . Behold the handmaid of the Lord . . ." (Luke 1:38). From that moment, and during the intervening years, there was always a question about her virginity. People actually raised questions about Jesus. She is really saying, "Here is Your opportunity to perform a miracle and demonstrate that I am accurate when I said that You were virgin born and that You are the One whom I have claimed You are." Jesus gives her a very clear answer.

Jesus saith unto her, Woman, what have I to do with thee? mine hour is not yet come [John 2:4].

His implication is, "This is not the occasion. I'll clear your name, but not here."

When He was hanging on the cross and the mother of Jesus was standing beneath that cross, you remember that He looked down and said to her, "Woman, behold thy son!" (John 19:26). At that time His hour had come. In three days He would come back from the dead. When the disciples met in an upper room after His resurrection and ascension, Mary could look around, for she was there, and she could say to each of those disciples, "I told you that He was the Son of God!" Paul says that He is ". . . declared to be the Son of God with power, according to the spirit of holiness, by the resurrection from the dead" (Rom. 1:4).

Here she is asking Him to do something that will demonstrate who He is to clear her name. He tells her that He is going to do just that—He will clear her name—but that the hour has not yet come. That hour did come! His resurrection proves who He is. And don't forget that the Resurrection proves the virgin birth of Christ. We tend to look at the virgin birth at Christmastime as an isolated fact. It is connected with His resurrection, friend, because He is who He claimed to be.

His mother saith unto the servants, Whatsoever he saith unto you, do it [John 2:5].

What good advice! I've always wanted to preach a Mother's Day sermon on this text, "Whatsoever he saith unto you, do it." My subject would be "A Mother's Advice." I never got around to it as a pastor, but it is good advice.

And there were set there six waterpots of stone, after the manner of the purifying of the Jews, containing two or three firkins apiece.

Jesus saith unto them, Fill the waterpots with water. And they filled them up to the brim [John 2:6–7].

Our attention is now drawn to these six water pots. They were used in ceremonial cleansing. Because this was a poor family, the pots were evidently beaten and battered and probably had been pushed in the back somewhere. They hoped when the wedding guests came that no one would notice them. I think our Lord must have embarrassed the family when He asked for those pots to be brought out. Then He tells them the exact procedure to follow, and they filled them to the brim.

And he saith unto them, Draw out now, and bear unto the governor of the feast. And they bare it.

When the ruler of the feast had tasted the water that was made wine, and knew not whence it was: (but the servants which drew the water knew;) the governor of the feast called the bridegroom,

CONTENTS

JOHN—Chapters 1—10

PREFACE

The radio broadcasts of the Thru the Bible Radio five-year program were transcribed, edited, and published first in single-volume paperbacks to accommodate the radio audience.

There has been a minimal amount of further editing for this publication. Therefore, these messages are not the word-for-word recording of the taped messages which went out over the air. The changes were necessary to accommodate a reading audience rather than a listening audience.

These are popular messages, prepared originally for a radio audience. They should not be considered a commentary on the entire Bible in any sense of that term. These messages are devoid of any attempt to present a theological or technical commentary on the Bible. Behind these messages is a great deal of research and study in order to interpret the Bible from a popular rather than from a scholarly (and too-often boring) viewpoint.

We have definitely and deliberately attempted "to put the cookies on the bottom shelf so that the kiddies could get them."

The fact that these messages have been translated into many languages for radio broadcasting and have been received with enthusiasm reveals the need for a simple teaching of the whole Bible for the masses of the world.

I am indebted to many people and to many sources for bringing this volume into existence. I should express my especial thanks to my secretary, Gertrude Cutler, who supervised the editorial work; to Dr. Elliott R. Cole, my associate, who handled all the detailed work with the publishers; and finally, to my wife Ruth for tenaciously encouraging me from the beginning to put my notes and messages into printed form.

Solomon wrote, ". . . of making many books there is no end; and much study is a weariness of the flesh" (Eccl. 12:12). On a sea of books that flood the marketplace, we launch this series of THRU THE BIBLE with the hope that it might draw many to the one Book, The Bible.

J. VERNON McGEE

The Gospel According to
JOHN

INTRODUCTION

It is generally assumed that the Gospel of John is easy to under-stand. Often you hear the cliché, "The Gospel of John is the *simple* Gospel." And the simplicity of the language has deceived a great many folk. It is written in monosyllabic and disyllabic words. Let me lift out a couple of verses to illustrate. Notice how simple these words are: "He came unto his own, and his own received him not. But as many as received him, to them gave he power to become the sons of God, even to them that believe on his name" (John 1:11–12).

We have no problem with the words themselves, but actually we're dealing here with the most profound Gospel. Take an expression like this: "ye in me, and I in you" which appears in John 14:20. Seven words—one conjunction, two prepositions and four pronouns—and you could ask any child in the fourth grade the meaning of any one of those words and he could give you a definition. But you put them together—"ye in me, and I in you"—and neither the most profound theologian nor the greatest philosopher has ever been able to probe the depths of their meaning. "Ye in me" we know means salvation; "and I in you" means sanctification, but beyond that none of us can go very far. We think, sometimes, because we know the meaning of words that we know what is being said. The words are simple, but the meaning is deep.

Jerome said of John's Gospel, "John excels in the depths of divine mysteries." And no truer statement was ever made. Dr. A. T. Pierson put it like this, "It touches the heart of Christ."

Though it is assumed that John is the simple Gospel, it's not always assumed that the apostle John is the author of it. The Baur-Tübingen School in Germany years ago began an attack upon the Gospel of John. And this has been a place where the liberal has really had a field day. I took a course in seminary (even in my day) on the authorship of the Gospel of John. The professor finally concluded the course by saying he thought John was the author. A wag in the class remarked, "Well, I believed John wrote it before I started the class and I believe it now, so I just wasted a semester!" Let me assure you that we are not going to waste time here relative to the authorship of this Gospel other than to mention two statements that make it quite obvious that John is the writer of it.

One of the reasons it was felt that John might not be the writer was because Papias (I've quoted him now for each of the Gospels) was thought to have never mentioned the authorship of John. But Professor Tischendorf, the German who found the Codex Sinaiticus, which is probably our best manuscript of the Old Testament, down in Saint Catherine's Monastery in the Sinaitic peninsula, was working in the Vatican library when he came upon an old manuscript that has a quotation from Papias in which it was made clear that John was the author of this Gospel. I personally wouldn't want any better authority than that. Also, Clement of Alexandria, who lived about A.D. 200, makes the statement that John was persuaded by friends and also moved by the Spirit of God to write a spiritual Gospel. And I believe that the Gospel of John is that spiritual Gospel. In my mind there's not a shadow of doubt that John is the author.

However, the more significant question is: Why did John write his Gospel? It was the last one written, probably close to A.D. 100. All the other apostles were dead, the writers of the New Testament were all gone, and he alone was left. In an attempt to answer this question we find again a diversity of theories. There are those who say that it was written to meet the first heresy of the church which was Gnosticism. The Gnostics believed that Jesus was God but not man at all, that the apostles only thought they saw Him, but actually did not. And Irenaeus expressly makes the statement that the purpose of John was to confute the Gnostic Cerinthus. But Tholuck makes it very clear that

And saith unto him, Every man at the beginning doth set forth good wine; and when men have well drunk, then that which is worse: but thou hast kept the good wine until now [John 2:8–10].

We don't want to get diverted here by arguing whether this wine was intoxicating or not. Very candidly, that is not the issue here at all. If you think you can make something out of this, you're entirely wrong.

Notice there is something omitted here. Where is the bride? I don't find her anywhere. And what did the bride wear? That's the most important part of our weddings. Now I've officiated at many weddings, hundreds of weddings during my ministry, and I've seen many brides come down the aisle. I've learned in the course of time that when I come in at the beginning, nobody is particularly interested in the preacher. Then the bridegroom comes in, and, very candidly, not many are interested in him. The only one who smiles at him is his mother. Then the bride comes down the aisle, and everybody looks. Now what did this bride at Cana wear? We don't know. Why? Because Jesus and those empty water pots are the important things here.

Friend, here is something wonderful. He took empty water pots and He had them filled with water. Then as they ladled out the water, I think the miracle took place. When they took the water and served it to the guests, it became wine.

This holds a great spiritual lesson for you and me. Jesus uses us as water pots today. We're just beaten and battered water pots. We're not attractive and ought to be pushed to the side and covered up. But He wants to use us. He wants to fill us with water. What is the water? The water is the Word of God, friend. He wants to fill you and me with the water of the Word of God. Then, after He fills us with the water of the Word of God, He wants us to ladle it out. When we ladle it out—I don't know how to explain it—but when the water leaves the water pots and gets to those for whom it is destined, it becomes wine. It becomes the wine of joy through the working of the Holy Spirit. We are told, "And be not drunk with wine, wherein is excess; but be filled with the Spirit" (Eph. 5:18). The Holy Spirit takes that water and performs a miracle in the life of an individual. Although I cannot explain it, I often see it take place. I have right here on my desk a dozen letters that have come in recently from people who have been saved by just hearing the Word of God through my radio program. Now, I don't understand it. I'm just an old water pot, and I've got a little of the water of the Word inside me. As I ladle it out, it becomes the wine of joy to folk who receive it.

Years ago when I was speaking to the Hollywood Christian group, there was a couple there who had been saved out of a night club. They said they were going to use their talent for Jesus. Well, I didn't like that. I asked them afterward what kind of a talent they used in a night club that Jesus could use. They stumbled around with an answer; so I said, "Look, when you and I came to Jesus, He didn't get anything but sinners. He got old battered water pots." So I told them about these water pots at Cana. I told them Jesus wanted to fill their lives with the Word of God, the water, and then wanted to ladle it out. I said that when the Holy Spirit ladled it out, it would become the wine of joy in their own lives and would bring a new desire and the joy of life into the life of any believer who would trust Him. They accepted that advice, and we remained good friends. Several years ago I met them on a street in Chicago. We saw each other coming. When they got within earshot, he said to me, "Here come a couple of old beaten up water pots." I want to say this: God has used them but not with the talent that was used in the night club. He filled them with the water of the Word of Life.

Friend, this is the great message that is here for you and me. He wants to fill us with the Word of God and then ladle it out.

After this he went down to Capernaum, he, and his mother, and his brethren, and his disciples: and they continued there not many days [John 2:12].

This is probably referring to that time when His hometown would not accept Him. When He went into the synagogue and read from Isaiah, they said, ". . . Is not this Joseph's son?" (Luke 4:22). They probably would have destroyed Him at that time. So he moved His headquarters to Capernaum, and, as far as I can tell, that continued to be His head-quarters during His ministry of three years.

JESUS CLEANSES THE TEMPLE DURING PASSOVER
IN JERUSALEM (First Word)

And the Jews' passover was at hand, and Jesus went up to Jerusalem [John 2:13].

Here we have another geographical point. He started out at Cana of Galilee, went to Capernaum, and is now in Jerusalem.

Notice that John labels this feast the "Jews' passover." It is no longer the ". . . LORD's passover . . ." (Exod. 12:27). It is the Jews' passover—merely a religious feast, quite meaningless, just a ritual to go through. The One of whom the Passover speaks has now come. ". . . For even Christ our passover is sacrificed for us" (1 Cor. 5:7).

Our Lord went up to Jerusalem. This was not at the beginning of His public ministry but probably at the end of the first year. All males were required to go to Jerusalem three times a year, at the time of the Feast of Passover, at the Feast of Pentecost, and at the Feast of Tabernacles. He went up for the Passover which was about April the fourteenth. So you see that John gears this into the geography and into the calendar.

Now we find that He cleanses the temple. He did this twice. One cleansing was at the beginning of His ministry and one again at the end of His ministry.

And found in the temple those that sold oxen and sheep and doves, and the changers of money sitting [John 2:14].

They were selling animals and selling doves and changing money. It is quite interesting that they would not accept any kind of money except the temple money there; no other kind could be used or offered. So they had an exchange place, and they made a good profit by making the exchange of coins. When I came back from Venezuela some time ago, I came back with some Venezuelan money that I wanted to get rid of because I couldn't spend it here. There was an exchange place in the airport, and I went up there and told them that I wanted to change it for American money. Believe me, friend, I didn't get as much as when I made the trade the other way around; that is, exchanging American money for the Venezuelan money. Now that is the way they did here at the temple, you see.

Why did they have such a system? Why did they do this? Because they were making religion easy. They would take the Roman coinage, which had an effigy of Caesar and the imprint of paganism on it, and they would exchange that for Jewish coinage which could be used in the temple. So they were there for the convenience of the worshipers. Also, they changed large coins into smaller ones. Not only did they make religion easy, but they also made religion cheap. I recognize that we ought not to overemphasize money in the church and should not beg, but I'll tell you something that is more intolerable than that. Some people treat the church and the cause of Christ as something so cheap that at times it becomes necessary to sound an alarm.

They were also selling animals. There was a lot of traffic in those sacrificial animals. It was work and expense to raise those sheep and oxen, and somebody would have to do it for a price. It was very easy for all this to become a religious racket. Today we have that problem with us also.

And when he had made a scourge of small cords, he drove them all out of the temple, and the sheep, and the oxen; and poured out the changers' money, and overthrew the tables;

And said unto them that sold doves, Take these things hence; make not my Father's house an house of merchandise.

And his disciples remembered that it was written, The zeal of thine house hath eaten me up [John 2:15–17].

I tell you, the Lord was rough. There is no question about that. I don't like the pictures we have of an anemic-looking Christ. The artists don't seem to realize who He was.

The disciples remembered the verse from Psalm 69:9. This psalm is quoted seventeen times in the New Testament and is one of the six most quoted psalms in the New Testament. It is quoted again in John 15:25 and 19:28–29. The other psalms which are frequently quoted are Psalms 2, 22, 89, 110, and 118.

> **Then answered the Jews and said unto him, What sign shewest thou unto us, seeing that thou doest these things?**
>
> **Jesus answered and said unto them, Destroy this temple, and in three days I will raise it up [John 2:18–19].**

The word that He used for destroy is *luo* which means "to untie." He is, of course, referring to His own human body.

> **Then said the Jews, Forty and six years was this temple in building, and wilt thou rear it up in three days? [John 2:20].**

The temple at that time was Herod's temple. It was still in the process of being built, and it had already been under construction for forty-six years.

There is a specific use of words in the Greek here that I want you to see. In verses 14 and 15, when it tells of Jesus cleansing the temple, the word used for temple is *hieron* which refers to the temple as a whole. Specifically, it was the outer court of the temple which Jesus cleansed. The word Jesus uses in verse 19 and the Jews repeat in verse 20 is *naos* which refers to the inner sanctuary of the temple. This word can also be used in reference to the body as Paul does in 1 Corinthians 6:19 when he says that the holy place today is not a temple made with hands but that our body is the temple (*naos*) of the Holy Spirit. The Jews were asking the Lord whether He really meant that He would destroy this temple, but, of course, our Lord meant the temple of His body.

But he spake of the temple of his body [John 2:21].

Jesus said that if they destroyed this temple, He would "raise it up." The word He used was *egeirō*, which John uses five times in his Gospel. Its actual meaning is "to wake up" and, each time the word is used, it refers to awaking from the dead. Paul used the same word in his sermon in Antioch of Pisidia where he used it four times. It refers to the resurrection of Christ, and it refers to the resurrection of believers also. It is used in reference to the restoration to life of Lazarus. It was a "waking up." That is the picture which we have in this word *egeirō*. That is precisely what He meant when He spoke of the temple of His body. But His disciples didn't understand that, and it was not until after His resurrection that they recalled it and referred to it.

When therefore he was risen from the dead, his disciples remembered that he had said this unto them; and they believed the scripture, and the word which Jesus had said [John 2:22].

JESUS INTERVIEWS NICODEMUS IN JERUSALEM
(Second Word)

Now we are coming to something that is intensely interesting. Actually, we should read from verse 23 right on into chapter 3 where we have the story of Nicodemus. All of this took place in Jerusalem during the time of the Passover.

Now when he was in Jerusalem at the passover, in the feast day, many believed in his name, when they saw the miracles which he did [John 2:23].

A great many folk read that and say, "My, isn't it wonderful that people were believing on Him." But it wasn't wonderful, friend, because theirs was not saving faith at all. They merely nodded in assent when they saw the miracles that He did. So notice what follows.

> **But Jesus did not commit himself unto them, because he knew all men,**
>
> **And needed not that any should testify of man: for he knew what was in man [John 2:24–25].**

The language that is used here is saying that He did not believe in them. You see, they believed in Him, but He didn't believe in them. In other words, to put it very frankly, their faith was not a saving faith, which He realized, of course. He knew what was in their hearts.

This is always a grave danger today for those who say they believe in Jesus. What do you *mean* when you say you believe in Jesus? Do you mean that you believe in the facts of the gospel? The important question is: Do you *trust Him* as your Savior who died for your sins? Was He raised for *your* justification? Is He your only hope of heaven?

This crowd was interested, and when they saw Him perform miracles, they believed. They had to—they *saw* the miracles. But Jesus didn't believe in them. He knew their belief was not genuine "because he knew all men." He knew what was in the human heart. He didn't need anyone to testify to Him of man because He knew what was in man.

In other words, the Lord Jesus didn't commit Himself unto the mob there. The great company believed on Him, but He didn't entrust Himself to them. When Nicodemus came to Him at night, our Lord did commit Himself unto him because this man's faith was genuine.

It is unfortunate that the movement here is broken by a chapter break.

CHAPTER 3

THEME: Jesus interviews Nicodemus in Jerusalem (second word)

JESUS INTERVIEWS NICODEMUS IN JERUSALEM
(Second Word)

This is an instance where the chapter break is unfortunate; so we will put it together without the break.

> **But Jesus did not commit himself unto them, because he knew all men,**
>
> **And needed not that any should testify of man: for he knew what was in man.**
>
> **There was a man of the Pharisees, named Nicodemus, a ruler of the Jews [John 2:24—3:1].**

This man is set apart from the mob. Our Lord didn't trust the mob because He knew their faith was not genuine. But this man Nicodemus is a genuine man. Let's get acquainted with him.

Three things are said about him here. The first thing is that he was a man of the Pharisees. That means that he belonged to the best group in Israel. They believed in the inspiration of the Old Testament, they believed in the coming of the Messiah, they believed in miracles, and they believed in the Resurrection. He was a man of the Pharisees, and his name was Nicodemus—we are given his name. And he was a ruler of the Jews. This tells us of the three masks that this man wore.

This is a picture of modern man if there ever was one. Nicodemus was a man of the Pharisees when he met with them. When he was in their midst, he was just one of them. He more or less let down his guard. Then, when he went out from the Pharisees and walked down the street, people would see him coming and would step off the sidewalk. He would be wearing his robe and his phylacteries and prayer shawl, and they would say, "My, that is the ruler, Nicodemus. He's an outstanding man. He's a ruler of the Jews." So he would adopt an altogether different attitude with them. But his name was Nicodemus, and down underneath these two masks that he wore, he was just plain, little old "Nicky."

There are many men who live like this today. There's many a man who is a businessman and president of a corporation. He goes into the office in the morning and those in the office speak to him and they call him, "Mister," and they bow and scrape to him. Although they think they know him, they don't really. Then he leaves his office and sees several of his customers that morning and when they ask him about business, he says, "Oh, business is great." Then he goes to his club at noon for lunch. The minute he steps inside the club, he's a different man. He's not Mister So-and-So, the president of a corporation, but now he's just plain old Joe Dokes. They play golf with him, they think they know him, and they call him by his first name. He adopts a different attitude with them. It is a different relationship. They ask him about business and he tells them, "Oh, business is great." Then in the evening, when the work is done, he goes home. He opens the door to his home, steps in and takes off his coat, and drops down into a chair. He's an altogether different man. His wife comes in and looks at him as he sits there dejected with both of his masks off now. He's no longer the businessman, the head of a corporation, and he's no longer one of the fellows at the club. Now he's just plain little old "Joe." His wife asks him, "What's the matter, Joe? Is business bad?" He replies, "Business is rotten." This is who he really is.

The same came to Jesus by night, and said unto him, Rabbi, we know that thou art a teacher come from God: for no man can do these miracles that thou doest, except God be with him [John 3:2].

This man, Nicodemus, comes to the Lord Jesus with a mask on. He says, "*we* know." Who is we? The Pharisees. He comes as a man of the Pharisees. He is wearing that mask.

He comes with a genuine compliment. He's no hypocrite. He says that we Pharisees have agreed that You are a teacher come from God. I think that he came to talk about the Kingdom of God. The Pharisees wanted to establish the kingdom and throw off the yoke of Rome, but they had no way of doing it. Here comes this One who is popular—with the multitudes following Him wherever He goes—so the Pharisees want to hitch their little wagon to His star. Since He has come from the country up in Galilee and they think He doesn't know how to deal with these politicians as they do, they want to combine forces. So Nicodemus comes, acknowledging that Jesus is a teacher come from God.

The proof that he points to is the miracles Jesus performed. He had to recognize the miracles. Please notice that no one doubted the miracles of our Lord—not in that day! You've got to be a professor in a seminary today, removed by two thousand years and several thousand miles from the land where it all took place, and then you can doubt the miracles. But you will not find that either the friends of Jesus or His enemies ever doubted His miracles.

Jesus answered and said unto him, Verily, verily, I say unto thee, Except a man be born again, he cannot see the kingdom of God [John 3:3].

This is the reason I think he came to talk about the kingdom of God. I see no other reason why our Lord would almost abruptly interrupt him and say to him, "The thing is, you can't even *see* the kingdom of God except you've been born again." Now here is a man, a Pharisee, who is religious to his fingertips, and yet our Lord told him he couldn't see the kingdom of God except he be born again. If this man came to talk about the kingdom and the establishing of it, which I think he did, then certainly this statement of our Lord detoured him. So now he drops the mask of the man of the Pharisees, but he is still a ruler of the Jews.

Nicodemus saith unto him, How can a man be born when he is old? can he enter the second time into his mother's womb, and be born? [John 3:4].

Jesus had said he must be born again. The Greek word for "again" is *anothen* which means "from above." This man Nicodemus couldn't think of anything but a physical birth. He immediately dropped the condescending mask of the Pharisee and asked how this could be. Our Lord wasn't speaking of a physical birth at all. He was speaking about a spiritual birth. But Nicodemus couldn't understand about a spiritual birth. The reason was that he had no spiritual capacity to comprehend it.

Jesus answered, Verily, verily, I say unto thee, Except a man be born of water and of the Spirit, he cannot enter into the kingdom of God [John 3:5].

Now what does it mean to be born of water and of the Spirit? There are those who think that to be born of water is a reference to water baptism. But this would be a strange expression if it did refer to that. Then, there have been several very fine Christian doctors who interpret "born of water" as the physical birth which is a birth in water; that is, the child in the womb is in water. I don't think that is what is meant here at all. He wasn't talking about the difference between natural birth and spiritual birth, but He was talking about *how* a man could be born "from above" or "born again."

As we saw in chapter 2, water is symbolic of the Word of God. We will find later in this book that Jesus says, "Sanctify them through thy truth: *thy word* is truth" (John 17:17, italics mine). There is a cleansing, sanctifying power in the Word. In John 15:3 Jesus says, "Now ye are clean through the *word* which I have spoken unto you" (italics mine). The Word of God is likened unto water again and again. We believe that "born of water and of the Spirit" means that a person must be born again by the Holy Spirit using the Scripture. We believe, very definitely, that no one could be born again without the Word of God applied by the Spirit of God. One today is born from above by the use of water, which is the Word of God, and the Spirit, the Holy Spirit, making it real to the heart.

There are three outstanding conversions in the Book of Acts. They have been given to us, I think, primarily as illustrations. There is the conversion of the Ethiopian eunuch, the conversion of Cornelius, and the conversion of Paul. These three men are representatives of the three families of Noah: the son of Shem, the son of Ham, and the son of Japheth. In each of these three cases, the Word of God was used by the Spirit of God for their conversions. God's method seems to be the Word of God, used by the Spirit of God, given through a man of God. I am confident that our Lord, saying that one must be born of water and of the Spirit, referred to the Spirit of God using the Word of God. Without this, Nicodemus could not enter into the kingdom of God.

That which is born of the flesh is flesh; and that which is born of the Spirit is spirit [John 3:6].

God does not intend to change the flesh, meaning this old nature which you and I have. The fact of the matter is that it can't be changed. The Word of God has much to say about this. The old nature is at war with God. "Because the carnal mind is enmity against God: for it is not subject to the law of God, neither indeed can be. So then they that are in the flesh cannot please God" (Rom. 8:7–8). God has no program for our old nature, to retrieve it or improve it or develop it or save it. That old nature is to go down into the grave with us. And, if the Lord comes before we go down into the grave, we are to be *changed* in the twinkling of an eye, which means we will get rid of that old nature. It can never be made obedient to God. "That which is born of the flesh is flesh." That is an axiom. God does not intend to save the flesh at all. This old nature must be replaced by the new nature. The spiritual birth is necessary so that you and I may be given a new nature, friend.

Now notice that Nicodemus who had been hiding behind the mask, "ruler of the Jews," will be losing it.

Marvel not that I said unto thee, Ye must be born again.

The wind bloweth where it listeth, and thou hearest the sound thereof, but canst not tell whence it cometh, and whither it goeth: so is every one that is born of the Spirit [John 3:7–8].

Jesus is saying, "You can't tell where the wind comes from and you can't tell where it is going." The air currents and the winds are something that man still doesn't control. The wind blows where it wills. We can't detour it, and we can't change it. There is an attempt being made to seed down the hurricanes in the Gulf of Mexico and the Caribbean area, but so far we haven't tamed the wind.

Although we can't control the wind, we surely can tell when it's blowing. You and I can be standing out on the street and you can say to me, "The wind is blowing!" I answer, "How do you know?" You would reply, "Look at that tree up there, see how the leaves are blowing, and notice how the tree is bending over." We can tell when the wind is blowing.

Now, friend, I don't know how to explain to you the spiritual birth. I know there are a lot of books being published that claim to explain it, but the difference between the authors and me is that they don't seem to know that they don't know, while I am willing to admit that I don't know. "The wind bloweth where it listeth . . . so is every one that is born of the Spirit." Although we don't quite understand it, it illustrates the way one is born of the Spirit. I can't tell you exactly how the Spirit of God operates, but I can surely tell when He is moving in the lives and hearts of His people. That's exactly what our Lord is saying here.

Our Lord has gotten rid of the two masks. The man who stands before Him is no longer the man of the Pharisees and he is no longer the ruler of the Jews. Who is he? Let's see what the verse says.

Nicodemus answered and said unto him, How can these things be? [John 3:9].

Now he stands there, just plain, little old "Nicky." He's wondering how these things can be, and our Lord is going to talk to him very plainly. By the way, you and I can put up our masks before each other, and there are many people today who use them. When they are with a certain crowd, they act a certain way. The mask, friend, hides just what we really are. When we come to the Lord Jesus, we have to take off all our masks. We can't use them there. You have to be the real "you." You have to come just as you are; then Jesus will deal with you that way. And this is the way He will deal with this man Nicodemus.

Jesus answered and said unto him, Art thou a master of Israel, and knowest not these things? [John 3:10].

That's gentle satire that our Lord is using here. He is saying to this man, "You are a ruler in Israel and acting as if I were telling you something that couldn't be true, because if it were true, you would have known about it." And then Jesus asks, "Don't you know these things, Nicodemus?"

Verily, verily, I say unto thee, We speak that we do know, and testify that we have seen; and ye receive not our witness.

If I have told you earthly things, and ye believe not, how shall ye believe, if I tell you of heavenly things?

And no man hath ascended up to heaven, but he that came down from heaven, even the Son of man which is in heaven [John 3:11–13].

He tells Nicodemus that he hasn't received His witness even as it was spoken to him.

Then He goes on to show that there is a tremendous movement which is set forth here in the Gospel of John. I called attention in the Introduction to the saying of our Lord in John 16:28, "I came forth from the Father, and am come into the world: again, I leave the world, and go to the Father." And now He says, "No man hath ascended up to heaven." That is the answer to those today who feel that Elijah and Enoch went to heaven when they were translated. I don't think so because up to this point the Lord Jesus says that no man hath ascended up to heaven, but He that came down from heaven, even the Son of Man which is in heaven. In other words, He is saying that He is the only One who can speak about heaven because He is the only One who has ascended up to heaven. Now it is true that there are a host of folk who have gone to heaven after Christ, but in the Old Testament when a saint of God died, one of God's own, he went to a place that is called Paradise or Abraham's Bosom—our Lord called it that (see Luke 16:22). It was not until after Christ died and ascended to heaven and led captivity captive that He took those who were in Paradise into the presence of God in heaven. Since then, for the child of God, it has always been ". . . absent from the body . . . present with the Lord" (2 Cor. 5:8). But when Jesus was here, no other man had ascended to heaven.

> **And as Moses lifted up the serpent in the wilderness, even so must the Son of man be lifted up:**
>
> **That whosoever believeth in him should not perish, but have eternal life [John 3:14–15].**

When Moses lifted up that brass serpent on a pole because of God's judgment upon the sin of the people, all they had to do for healing was to look to it. As Moses lifted up the serpent, so Christ is going to be lifted up. That serpent, you see, represented the sin of the people. And Christ was made sin for us on the Cross because He bore our sin there. As Moses lifted up the serpent in the wilderness, even so must the Son of Man be lifted up.

Now our Lord repeats to Nicodemus probably the most familiar words we have in the Bible:

> **For God so loved the world, that he gave his only begotten Son, that whosoever believeth in him should not perish, but have everlasting life [John 3:16].**

There are two things that we need to note here. One is that we *must* be born again. The other is that the Son of Man *must* be lifted up. They are related. It takes the death of Christ and the resurrection of Christ— He must be lifted up. Since He has been lifted up, since He bore our penalty, the Spirit of God can regenerate us. And we *must* be born again—that is the only way God can receive us.

The motivation for all of this is that God so *loved* the world. God never saved the world by love, which is the mistaken thinking of today. It doesn't say that God's love saved the world, because the love of God could never save a sinner. God does not save by love, friends. *God saves by grace!* "For by grace are ye saved through faith; and that not of yourselves: it is the gift of God: not of works, lest any man should boast" (Eph. 2:8–9). Now, how does God save? God saves by grace. But God so *loved* the world, that He *gave* His only begotten Son that whoever (you can write your name in here and I can write mine) believes in Him should not perish, but have everlasting life. Notice that with the word *believe* is the little preposition *in* which means to believe *in* Christ. That is, we trust Him as the One who bore the penalty for our sins. This is a personal thing. We must each believe that He died in our place and in our stead. My friend, you must believe that He died for you.

> **For God sent not his Son into the world to condemn the world; but that the world through him might be saved.**
>
> **He that believeth on him is not condemned: but he that believeth not is condemned already, because he hath not believed in the name of the only begotten Son of God [John 3:17–18].**

We see here that, when Jesus came the first time, He was not a judge. He made that very clear to the man who wanted Him to give a judgment between himself and his brother. He said, ". . . Man, who made me a judge or a divider over you?" (Luke 12:14). He didn't come as a Judge the first time. He came as the Savior. He will come the next time as the Judge. But now He says that God didn't send Him into the world to condemn the world, but that the world through Him might be saved. Whoever does not believe in Him is condemned. Friend, if you don't believe, you are already condemned. Why? Because "he hath not believed in the name of the only begotten Son of God." That wonderful name is Jesus—His name is Jesus because He is the Savior of the world. Anyone who will believe in that name is no longer under condemnation but has everlasting life.

Remember that He is talking to Nicodemus, a Pharisee. The Pharisees believed that the Messiah, when He came, would be a judge. The Old Testament presented two aspects of the coming of the Messiah. One was His coming as a Savior, coming to die, coming to pay a penalty; the other was His coming as the Judge. They reasoned that the Messiah would be a judge when He came because the Old Testament presents that aspect. In Psalm 2:9 we read, "Thou shalt break them with a rod of iron. . . ." Daniel speaks of Him as a judge of the whole world (Dan. 7:13–14). Psalm 45 talks about His ruling the world in righteousness, and Isaiah 11 and Isaiah 42 speak of His judgments in righteousness. The Lord Jesus is making it very clear to Nicodemus that God sent not His Son *this time* to judge the world, but that the world through Him might be saved. The "world" is the Greek word *kosmos*—God's redemptive purpose embraces the entire world. He did not come to condemn or to judge the world but to save the world.

In Christ there is no condemnation. Those who are not in Christ are *already* condemned. There are a great many who feel that the world is on trial today. It is not. The world is lost. You and I live in a lost world, and we'll not wait until the final judgment to see that we are lost. Our position is something like a man who is in prison being asked whether or not he will accept a pardon. That is the gospel. It is not telling a man that he is on trial. He is already condemned. He is already in prison waiting for execution. But the gospel tells him a pardon is offered to him. The point is, will you accept the pardon? How wonderfully clear that is. The gospel is to save those who are already lost.

> **And this is the condemnation, that light is come into the world, and men loved darkness rather than light, because their deeds were evil.**
>
> **For every one that doeth evil hateth the light, neither cometh to the light, lest his deeds should be reproved.**
>
> **But he that doeth truth cometh to the light, that his deeds may be made manifest, that they are wrought in God [John 3:19–21].**

This is the judgment, you see, of the world. The day that the world crucified Christ—on that day the world made a decision. It must now be judged by God. The condemnation, or the judgment, is that light is come into the world, but because men's deeds were habitually evil, they loved the darkness. Rats always scurry for a dark corner when light enters a room. Today I received a letter from a girl who said that, before she was saved, she never cared for our Bible-teaching program. Naturally, she did not want the light at all. Only those who turn to Christ want the light.

Notice that in this verse our Lord approaches so many things from the negative point. "For every one that doeth evil hateth the light, neither cometh to the light, lest his deeds should be reproved." We hear today of the power of positive thinking. Believe me, friend, there is a lot of power in negative thinking and negative speaking. Listen to other things He said. ". . . I came *not* to call the righteous, but sinners to repentance" and ". . . the Son of man came *not* to be ministered unto, but to minister, and to give his life a ransom for many" (Mark 2:17; 10:45, italics mine). "God sent *not* his Son into the world to condemn the world." And He says that every one that doeth evil hateth the light. In other words, whoever habitually practices what is wrong hates the light. "Light" and "truth" are used in the same way. "He that doeth truth cometh to the light." Error and darkness are always in contrast to light and truth. This ends His interview with Nicodemus.

TESTIMONY OF JOHN THE BAPTIST

After these things came Jesus and his disciples into the land of Judaea; and there he tarried with them, and baptized.

And John also was baptizing in Aenon near to Salim, because there was much water there: and they came, and were baptized.

For John was not yet cast into prison [John 3:22–24].

At this time, John was still able to preach ". . . the kingdom of heaven is at hand" (Matt. 3:2). It was after the Lord's temptation that John was cast into prison. The other Gospels tell us that.

> **Then there arose a question between some of John's disciples and the Jews about purifying.**
>
> **And they came unto John, and said unto him, Rabbi, he that was with thee beyond Jordan, to whom thou barest witness, behold, the same baptizeth, and all men come to him [John 3:25–26].**

This is a very interesting statement. The disciples of John, I would assume, are jealous. They are suggesting that he should not mention the name of Jesus. They feel it would be best if he didn't. And then they imply that he should not have borne witness to Him to begin with because all are going to Him—well, now, that is hyperbole—but it reveals they were jealous and were afraid John was going to lose all his followers.

Now this man John makes a very clear statement. There is not a jealous bone in the body of John.

> **John answered and said, A man can receive nothing, except it be given him from heaven.**
>
> **Ye yourselves bear me witness, that I said, I am not the Christ, but that I am sent before him.**
>
> **He that hath the bride is the bridegroom: but the friend of the bridegroom, which standeth and heareth him, rejoiceth greatly because of the bridegroom's voice: this my joy therefore is fulfilled.**
>
> **He must increase, but I must decrease [John 3:27–30].**

One cannot escape the tremendous force of this, friend. John the Baptist is the last of the Old Testament prophets. He is actually not in the church. He makes it clear here: "He that hath the bride. . . ." Who is the bride? The church. "He that hath the bride is the bridegroom." Then who is John? He is the friend of the Bridegroom. He will be present at the marriage supper of the Lamb, but he is not a part of the church by any means. He is the last of the Old Testament prophets who walks out of the Old Testament onto pages of the New Testament to announce the coming of the Messiah.

"A man can receive nothing, except it be given him from heaven." Again and again this truth will come out. Jesus said, "No man can come unto me, except it were given unto him of my Father" (John 6:65). How tremendous these statements are! And then John says that Christ must increase but that John must decrease. His ministry is now coming to an end.

> **He that cometh from above is above all: he that is of the earth is earthly, and speaketh of the earth: he that cometh from heaven is above all.**
>
> **And what he hath seen and heard, that he testifieth; and no man receiveth his testimony.**
>
> **He that hath received his testimony hath set to his seal that God is true.**
>
> **For he whom God hath sent speaketh the words of God: for God giveth not the Spirit by measure unto him.**
>
> **The Father loveth the Son, and hath given all things into his hand.**
>
> **He that believeth on the Son hath everlasting life: and he that believeth not the Son shall not see life; but the wrath of God abideth on him [John 3:31–36].**

John makes it very clear that the Lord Jesus Christ is superior, and he gives them this wonderful testimony concerning the Lord Jesus.

"He that believeth on the Son *hath* everlasting life." You have it right now! Friend, you couldn't have it any clearer than that. John the

Baptist preached the gospel, as you can see. He told the message that men are lost without Christ, but they have everlasting life through faith in Christ. What a testimony this man had. What a tremendous witness to the Lord Jesus Christ!

CHAPTER 4

THEME: *Jesus interviews the woman at the well in Sychar (third word); Jesus heals the nobleman's son in Capernaum (second work)*

Chapter 4 brings us to the very important incident in the ministry of our Lord as He goes through Samaria.

When therefore the Lord knew how the Pharisees had heard that Jesus made and baptized more disciples than John,

(Though Jesus himself baptized not, but his disciples,)

He left Judaea, and departed again into Galilee [John 4:1–3].

This, apparently, was immediately after the incident in chapter 3. It was in the month of December and probably near December 27. This was the time that John the Baptist was in prison. When John was imprisoned, Jesus left Judea and went back into Galilee.

Why did He retire from Judea? Well, He did not want to precipitate a crisis. You see, the Lord Jesus was moving according to schedule, a heavenly schedule set by the Father. He has made it very clear that He came to do the Father's will. Speaking of His own life, He said, "No man taketh it from me, but I lay it down of myself. I have power to lay it down, and I have power to take it again. This commandment have I received of my Father" (John 10:18). They can't touch Him until His time has come. When we reach the thirteenth chapter of John, we will see that His time had then come. "Now before the feast of the passover, when Jesus knew that his hour was come that he should depart out of this world unto the Father . . ." (John 13:1)—you see, He's moving on His Father's schedule, friend; He has come to do the Father's will.

So He departed again into Galilee. He went back up where His headquarters were, which, we believe, were in the city of Capernaum.

JESUS INTERVIEWS THE WOMAN AT THE WELL IN SYCHAR (Third Word)

And he must needs go through Samaria [John 4:4].

That word *must* attracts our attention. Why *must* He go through Samaria? In order to reach a certain woman. Listen to Him in verse 34, "My meat is to do the will of him that sent me, and to finish his work." He must go through Samaria because it is the Father's will for Him to go through Samaria. His destination, apparently, was Cana of Galilee where He had made the water into wine. There was a certain noble-man whose son was sick, and He is headed in that direction. But He must go through Samaria.

There were three routes He could have taken. He could have gone along the coast. There was a route there, and it is still there today, by the way. He could have gone through Peraea, which is up at the other side of Jordan. Or He could go through Samaria. Josephus tells us that, although the most direct route was through Samaria, the Jews didn't go that route due to the antipathy between the Jews and the Samaritans. However, our Lord went through Samaria.

> **Then cometh he to a city of Samaria, which is called Sychar, near to the parcel of ground that Jacob gave to his son Joseph [John 4:5].**

Joseph's tomb is nearby. At the fork of the old Roman road south of Sychar He meets the woman at the well. Mount Gerizim is to the northwest, and the synagogue of the Samaritans is on the slope of Mount Gerizim. I've been at that spot and have taken pictures there. This is the place to which our Lord comes.

> **Now Jacob's well was there. Jesus therefore, being wearied with his journey, sat thus on the well: and it was about the sixth hour [John 4:6].**

The sixth hour according to Roman time would be six o'clock in the evening, but we are following Jewish time here and the sixth hour was twelve noon. He was weary with His journey. How perfectly human He was. You see, John presents Him as the Son of God, as God manifest in the flesh. "The Word was made flesh" (John 1:14). Friend, although the language is simple, it expresses something that is overwhelming. Think of it! The God of eternity came down to this earth. The Word was made flesh and dwelled among us—He pitched His tent here among us. He went through Samaria and sat down at a well in order that He might reach this woman of Samaria!

The Samaritans were a group of poor people in that day.

> **There cometh a woman of Samaria to draw water: Jesus saith unto her, Give me to drink [John 4:7].**

This woman is obviously a dissolute woman. I think she is probably as common as pig tracks. She's rude and immoral. We would call her today a hussy or a broad, if you please.

What a contrast she is to the man, Nicodemus, we saw in the preceding chapter. And notice how differently our Lord deals with her. With Nicodemus, a man who was religious to his fingertips, our Lord was harsh and blunt, but see how gentle He is with this woman. He asks a favor of her. He appeals to her sympathy—He is thirsty and asks for a drink. What condescension on His part! He is the Water of Life and He asks her for water.

> **(For his disciples were gone away unto the city to buy meat.) [John 4:8].**

It is noon and His disciples have gone to the city to buy food. The fact that they were buying the Samaritans' food also reveals Jesus' total rejection of the Jewish prejudice which considered Samaritan food unclean, even as swine's flesh.

> **Then saith the woman of Samaria unto him, How is it that thou, being a Jew, askest drink of me, which am a**

woman of Samaria? for the Jews have no dealings with the Samaritans [John 4:9].

Twice she refuses His request. She's rude here, and insolent, impudent, and impertinent—she tosses her pert and saucy head. She makes this racial distinction. It is said that the Samaritans would sell to the Jews, but they wouldn't drink from the same vessel with them.

You see what our Lord is doing here. He is coming to the very lowest place to which He can come. But watch how the Lord deals with her. He is very skillful and sympathetic, but He also talks with her forcefully, faithfully, and factually. He doesn't give her a lecture on integration or civil rights. He isn't a candidate for some office. He just appeals to her womanly curiosity. He creates an interest and a thirst.

Jesus answered and said unto her, If thou knewest the gift of God, and who it is that saith to thee, Give me to drink; thou wouldest have asked of him, and he would have given thee living water [John 4:10].

As He appeals to her curiosity, her attitude immediately changes.

The woman saith unto him, Sir, thou hast nothing to draw with, and the well is deep: from whence then hast thou that living water?

Art thou greater than our father Jacob, which gave us the well, and drank thereof himself, and his children, and his cattle? [John 4:11–12].

The woman calls Him "Sir" which she had left out before. Then she was impudent and rude, but now there is a difference. The whole point here is that this woman is thinking in terms of the physical; her thinking could get no higher than the water level down in the well.

Notice that she identifies herself with Jacob. She does this purposely, as racially the Samaritans were Jacob's descendants who had intermarried with peoples from the north following the Assyrian captivity of Israel in 721 B.C.

> Jesus answered and said unto her, Whosoever drinketh
> of this water shall thirst again:
>
> But whosoever drinketh of the water that I shall give
> him shall never thirst; but the water that I shall give him
> shall be in him a well of water springing up into ever-
> lasting life [John 4:13–14].

Jesus makes it clear that He is not talking about water in Jacob's well.
Rather, He is making a contrast, you see. Today the crowds are going
to the water holes of this world, seeking satisfaction. They also are
constantly looking for the physical, not the spiritual satisfaction. But
now Jesus has created a desire in this woman's heart for the spiritual
water.

> The woman saith unto him, Sir, give me this water, that
> I thirst not, neither come hither to draw [John 4:15].

She's thirsty for spiritual water, but then her thinking goes right back
down into that well again.

> Jesus saith unto her, Go, call thy husband, and come
> hither [John 4:16].

This is the master stroke. Although the water is available for all, there
is a condition to be met—there must be a thirst, a need. She must,
therefore, recognize that she is a sinner. So our Lord says to her, "Go
call your husband." That is a touchy subject. She becomes flippant
again.

> The woman answered and said, I have no husband.
> Jesus said unto her, Thou hast well said, I have no hus-
> band:
>
> For thou hast had five husbands; and he whom thou now
> hast is not thy husband: in that saidst thou truly [John
> 4:17–18].

She was accurate about that. She had had five husbands, but she
didn't have one then. She was living with a man in adultery. Our Lord
insists that, when you come to Him, you must deal with sin. All se-
crets must come out before Him. Here was a sinner. One of the reasons
she was not so popular with the women of the town was because she
was too popular with the men of the town.

The woman was actually shocked into reverence. But then she
wanted to change the subject by opening a religious argument.

> **The woman saith unto him, Sir, I perceive that thou art
> a prophet.**
>
> **Our fathers worshipped in this mountain; and ye say,
> that in Jerusalem is the place where men ought to wor-
> ship [John 4:19–20].**

Now that will make a good religious argument, friend. Where are you
going to worship? In this mountain or in Jerusalem? That caused
many an argument in that day.

There are many people today who want to argue religion, but they
don't want to live it. I'm convinced that most of the superficiality in
our churches today is there as a cover-up of sin. Unfortunately our
churches are honey-combed with hypocrisy, a compromise with evil,
and a refusal to face up to sin. You know, it's easy to preach about the
sin of the Moabites which they committed about 4,000 years ago, but
what about our sins today? It was the brother of Henry Ward Beecher
who said, "I like a sermon where one man is the preacher and one
man is the congregation so that when the preacher says, 'Thou art the
man,' there's no mistaking whom he's talking about." There are many
ministers today who are afraid to preach on the sins of Christians.
This was confirmed to me several years ago. I was speaking in a summer conference on the first eight chapters of Romans. This is not often
used as a subject because Paul deals with sin. At first I could actually
feel a resentment. By the middle of the week, the Holy Spirit began to
break up hard hearts and a fellow who seemed to be the most pom-
pous and pious saint came to me wanting to confess his sins. I told

him not to confess them to me, but to go to the great High Priest, the Lord Jesus. He would hear him when he confessed, and He would forgive him. What a change took place in this man! At that same conference two ministers came to me, personally and privately, asking, "Do you preach like this in your own church?" Well, I did preach like that, but I found out there was a little cell of super-duper saints who liked to criticize the preacher so as to take the attention off themselves. They really wanted to be active—in fact, they wanted to run the church—but they did not want to deal with sin in their lives.

Our Lord did not avoid or sidestep the issue of personal sin. I believe that if you really have honest questions or doubts, the Lord will reveal the solution to you. And our Lord dealt with this woman on the question she had raised.

> **Jesus saith unto her, Woman, believe me, the hour cometh, when ye shall neither in this mountain, nor yet at Jerusalem, worship the Father.**
>
> **Ye worship ye know not what: we know what we worship: for salvation is of the Jews [John 4:21–22].**

The thing that was important to this woman was whether she should worship God in this mountain where the Samaritans worship Him, or should she worship Him in Jerusalem. Jesus told her the day was coming when He would not be worshiped in either place. Why?

> **But the hour cometh, and now is, when the true worshippers shall worship the Father in spirit and in truth: for the Father seeketh such to worship him.**
>
> **God is a Spirit: and they that worship him must worship him in spirit and in truth [John 4:23–24].**

It is irrelevant, therefore, where you worship God. It is not *where* but *how* you worship Him that is important. Our Lord answered her very adequately. God is a Spirit. You don't have to run to this place or that place. True worshipers worship Him in spirit and in truth.

> **The woman saith unto him, I know that Messias cometh, which is called Christ: when he is come, he will tell us all things [John 4:25].**

Even the Samaritans were looking for the Messiah to come. That is something that is very interesting. Today the second coming of Christ is believed and loved by those who are His. Those who are not really His, though church members, have a nagging feeling that He might come. Although they say they don't believe in His second coming, it still disturbs them.

An atheist in London several years ago made the statement that the thing that disturbed him was that the Bible might be true and that Jesus might come again. If He did, this man realized he would be in trouble. Believe me, he surely will be in trouble!

The woman now is profoundly interested, and there is a wistful longing in her heart.

> **The woman saith unto him, I know that Messias cometh, which is called Christ: when he is come, he will tell us all things.**
>
> **Jesus saith unto her, I that speak unto thee am he [John 4:25–26].**

How majestic and sublime this statement is! This woman is brought face to face now with the Savior of the world, the Messiah. Friend, this is my question to you today, whoever you are, wherever you are, and however you are: Have you come face to face with the Lord Jesus Christ as this woman did? I tell you, she found herself in His presence. "I that speak unto thee am he!"

> **And upon this came his disciples, and marvelled that he talked with the woman: yet no man said, What seekest thou? or, Why talkest thou with her?**
>
> **The woman then left her waterpot, and went her way into the city, and saith to the men,**

> **Come, see a man, which told me all things that ever I did: is not this the Christ? [John 4:27–29].**

The woman had turned in faith to the Lord Jesus, so now she rushes into the city to tell others. Notice that she doesn't talk to the women because she's not on speaking terms with them. Some of those men were involved with her, and they are very much interested in knowing whether He could tell all things that she had done. So here is what happened.

> **Then they went out of the city, and came unto him [John 4:30].**

The men came because of her witness. That is very important for us to see. The fact that she witnessed to others is evidence of her faith.

> **In the mean while his disciples prayed him, saying, Master, eat.**
>
> **But he said unto them, I have meat to eat that ye know not of.**
>
> **Therefore said the disciples one to another, Hath any man brought him aught to eat?**
>
> **Jesus saith unto them, My meat is to do the will of him that sent me, and to finish his work [John 4:31–34].**

The reason that He went through Samaria was to do the Father's will by reaching this woman.

> **Say not ye, There are yet four months, and then cometh harvest? behold, I say unto you, Lift up your eyes, and look on the fields; for they are white already to harvest.**
>
> **And he that reapeth receiveth wages, and gathereth fruit unto life eternal: that both he that soweth and he that reapeth may rejoice together.**

And herein is that saying true, One soweth, and another reapeth.

I sent you to reap that whereon ye bestowed no labour: other men laboured, and ye are entered into their labours [John 4:35–38].

Remember that this took place in December, and harvest in that area would be in April.

In this age in which we are living today, our business is to sow. I am attempting through the radio media to sow the Word of God. I hope that good churches will reap because I have sown. One pastor told me that because of the radio messages, he had received into his church over one hundred members. We are reaching a great many people who are members of liberal churches, but they want to know where to go to be taught the Word of God. This pastor said that because folk had listened to the broadcast and then realized that they wanted the Word of God, they had come to his church. They will join churches where the Word is taught. One sows and another reaps. I rejoice in that.

And many of the Samaritans of that city believed on him for the saying of the woman, which testified, He told me all that ever I did [John 4:39].

A great company was reached in Samaria through this woman with the "shady" past!

So when the Samaritans were come unto him, they besought him that he would tarry with them: and he abode there two days.

And many more believed because of his own word;

And said unto the woman, Now we believe, not because of thy saying: for we have heard him ourselves, and know that this is indeed the Christ, the Saviour of the world [John 4:40–42].

What a wonderful thing we see here. They came to the Living Water and they drank. The only condition was for them to thirst. You will never know that you thirst until you know that you are a sinner, friend. Isaiah cried, "Ho, every one that thirsteth, come ye to the waters . . ." (Isa. 55:1). Our Lord gave the same invitation: "If any man thirst, let him come unto me, and drink" (John 7:37). The Water of Life is for "any man." But the one condition is thirst. Many of the Samaritans came to Him, and they drank.

As many men came to Christ through the witness of the woman at Samaria, today many people are led to know Christ through the influence of another. In fact, it is the effect of one life upon other lives, the impact of one personality upon another, which often leads people to Christ. Some young people have remarkable parents, or one remarkable parent, and because of the influence of the parent they may come to Christ. They live in the light of that parent with no personal contact with Christ Himself. Then later they stumble and fall when the influence of the parent is gone. I've seen that happen again and again during my years as a pastor. It is a wonderful thing to exercise an influence on another for Christ, but don't let it stand there! See that the individual gets through to Christ in a personal relationship for himself. The Samaritans said, "Now we believe, not because of thy saying: for we have heard him ourselves, and know that this is indeed the Christ, the Saviour of the world."

JESUS HEALS THE NOBLEMAN'S SON IN CAPERNAUM (Second Work)

Now after two days he departed thence, and went into Galilee.

For Jesus himself testified, that a prophet hath no honour in his own country.

Then when he was come into Galilee, the Galilaeans received him, having seen all the things that he did at Jerusalem at the feast: for they also went unto the feast.

So Jesus came again into Cana of Galilee, where he made the water wine. And there was a certain nobleman, whose son was sick at Capernaum [John 4:43–46].

Notice the geography John gives us here again. Jesus leaves Samaria and goes into Galilee, and many Galileans believe on Him because they had seen Him at the feast and had watched the things He had done. Then He goes specifically to Cana of Galilee because there is a certain nobleman there whose son is way down in Capernaum.

When he heard that Jesus was come out of Judaea into Galilee, he went unto him, and besought him that he would come down, and heal his son: for he was at the point of death [John 4:47].

Here is a father who exercised faith in behalf of his son. This illustrates the thing we have just been saying. Make sure your own child has a *personal* contact with Jesus Christ. The essential thing would have been for the father to have brought the boy to Christ. I think that we have a right to claim our loved ones for Christ. We should exercise our own influence upon the lives of others. I believe that you've got to be a witness to your loved ones and that you've got to reveal in your own life that you have a living faith in Christ and that it works.

A man who was a member of the church I served in Los Angeles came to me one day, asking me to pray for the salvation of his son. Unfortunately, although he was an officer of the church, his life wasn't very good. The boy had walked out of the house, and I honestly couldn't blame the boy for it at all. The father wanted me to counsel with the boy and attempt to lead him to Christ. I very candidly told him that I wouldn't talk with the boy. I said, "You've served that boy 'roast preacher' for so long that he hasn't any use for me. You've done nothing but criticize. Now you've lost your influence with him, and I will pray that someone else will exert an influence on your boy and bring him to the Lord." Friend, if you are a parent, remember that your life exerts a powerful influence upon your children, both good and bad.

The nobleman came to Jesus asking Him to come down and heal his son who was at the point of death.

> **Then said Jesus unto him, Except ye see signs and won-ders, ye will not believe.**
>
> **The nobleman saith unto him, Sir, come down ere my child die.**
>
> **Jesus saith unto him, Go thy way; thy son liveth. And the man believed the word that Jesus had spoken unto him, and he went his way [John 4:48–50].**

This man protested that he was not just looking for signs and won-ders; he wanted his boy. That was all-important to him. Jesus re-sponded to this man's faith and He did heal the boy. That is wonderful.

However, it's too bad he didn't bring the boy into the presence of Christ. That was of the utmost importance. We hope he did so after the boy was well. The Samaritan woman, even though she had been a bad woman, brought the men face-to-face with the Lord Jesus.

You can influence someone that no preacher can reach. In fact, nobody else can reach that individual but you. You have influence over that individual. Be very sure that you bring him face to face with Christ.

> **And as he was now going down, his servants met him, and told him, saying, Thy son liveth.**
>
> **Then inquired he of them the hour when he began to amend. And they said unto him, Yesterday at the seventh hour the fever left him [John 4:51–52].**

It's difficult to be sure just what time John is using. According to Ro-man time this would have been about seven in the evening.

> **So the father knew that it was at the same hour, in the which Jesus said unto him, Thy son liveth: and himself believed, and his whole house.**

> **This is again the second miracle that Jesus did, when he was come out of Judaea into Galilee [John 4:53–54].**

The father claimed his whole household for Christ. They would each have to exert faith personally, but this man claimed them and would exert his influence for Christ.

The word for *miracle* here is actually the word *sign*. This is the second sign that Jesus did.

CHAPTER 5

THEME: *Jesus heals man at Pool of Bethesda (third work)*

JESUS HEALS MAN AT POOL OF BETHESDA
(Third Work)

Chapter 5 brings us to this very wonderful incident of the healing of the impotent man at the pool of Bethesda. Actually, in a sense, this miracle is the turning point in the ministry of Christ. You see, this miracle set the bloodhounds of hate on His track, and they never let up until they put Him to death on the cross.

Notice verse 16:

> **And therefore did the Jews persecute Jesus, and sought to slay him, because he had done these things on the sabbath day.**

> **But Jesus answered them, My Father worketh hitherto, and I work.**

> **Therefore the Jews sought the more to kill him, because he not only had broken the sabbath, but said also that God was his Father, making himself equal with God [John 5:16–18].**

You see, the clash with them was over the Sabbath Day; they never forgave Him for what He did on the Sabbath. They hated Him because He said, ". . . The sabbath was made for man, and not man for the sabbath" (Mark 2:27). The miracle that our Lord performed here really put murder into their hearts. They hated Him because of the Sabbath and because He made Himself equal with God.

"Making himself equal with God" is a clear-cut claim to deity. I have heard the liberals say that the Bible does not teach the deity of Christ. I don't know what those men are talking about. I feel they are either woefully ignorant or they are absolutely dishonest. You may disagree with the Lord Jesus, and you may disagree with the Bible, but how can you put any other construction on these plain words, "making himself equal with God"? If that isn't claiming deity, then I do not know how a person would be able to claim deity.

Now let's go back to the beginning of the chapter. It starts with a feast of the Jews. The question arises as to which feast this is. It is probably the Passover. There are three great feasts of the Jews: "Three times in a year shall all thy males appear before the LORD thy God in the place which he shall choose; in the feast of unleavened bread, and in the feast of weeks, and in the feast of tabernacles . . ." (Deut. 16:16). Since in John 2 we find the Passover, and in John 7 we find the Feast of Tabernacles, many have assumed that this feast is Pentecost. We are not told because that is not really the important thing here. I rather think it could be the Feast of Passover again.

> **After this there was a feast of the Jews; and Jesus went up to Jerusalem.**
>
> **Now there is at Jerusalem by the sheep market a pool, which is called in the Hebrew tongue Bethesda, having five porches.**
>
> **In these lay a great multitude of impotent folk, of blind, halt, withered, waiting for the moving of the water [John 5:1–3].**

Now it was really the sheep gate, not a market, where the pool was. The name of the pool was Bethesda which means "house of olives" or "house of mercy." It had five porches. In these lay a great multitude. The word *great* is not in the better manuscripts, but it doesn't change the meaning because a multitude is a great number anyway. "A multitude of *impotent* folk" means people without strength.

Many years ago when I was pastor in Pasadena, I went up one year to speak at the Preventorium where little fellows and girls who had weak lungs or tuberculosis were cared for. They presented an Easter program. There was one little fellow there who quoted this entire fifth chapter of John, all forty-seven verses. He made only one error and I always felt it wasn't much of an error. In verse 3, he quoted it like this, "In these lay a great multitude of *important* folk." Quite a few people smiled when he said that. I got to thinking about it and realized he was correct. They were important. One of them caused the Lord Jesus to come to this place, and any of the others could have turned to Him. They were important to Him.

The fourth verse of this chapter is not in the better manuscripts. To say this does not mean that I don't believe in the inerrancy of Scripture. I want to assure you that I do believe in the inerrancy of Scripture. Why in the world do you think that I teach the entire Bible? But I do think we should heed scholarship—fundamental, conservative scholarship which suggests that because it is not in the better manuscripts, it was put in by a scribe as a word of explanation. I believe it is factual, and it helps me understand why this crowd of impotent folk were here. But whether it belongs in Scripture or not is not worth an argument. To me it is not the essential thing because there is something far more important here. However, I did want to give this word of explanation.

For an angel went down at a certain season into the pool, and troubled the water: whosoever then first after the troubling of the water stepped in was made whole of whatsoever disease he had [John 5:4].

This is the explanation of why they were there. The belief was that an angel stirred the water at a certain season. I personally feel that a great many cures took place there that were psychological cures. There are a number of people today, just as there were then, who are sick in their minds, ignorant, and superstitious. There are quite a few who go to faith healers today who believe they get healed. There is always a question whether or not they were ever really sick. Another question is whether they stay permanently healed. My point is that the Lord Jesus Christ heals today just as He did at the pool of Bethesda, and that one is not healed by some moving of the water.

And a certain man was there, which had an infirmity thirty and eight years [John 5:5].

Our attention is directed to one man here. Whether he had been at the pool all that time we do not know. We are told that he was infirm for thirty-eight years and that apparently he moved with difficulty. I would judge he was the worst case there. Think of how frustrating it was for this poor fellow! Even if he hadn't been there for the thirty-eight years, he must have been there for several years. He must have been much older than thirty-eight years, and his condition was the result of his own sin. In verse 14 the Lord Jesus said to him, "Behold, thou art made whole: sin no more, lest a worse thing come unto thee." You can well imagine this poor fellow lying there, keeping his eyes on the water, waiting for the moving of the water. He would hope somehow or other to be the first one to get down in the water. But there had been disappointment after disappointment. He was in such a bad state that the others would always get into the water first. I'm sure he saw many cures there. People who were sick in their minds would be healed in their minds.

Our Lord apparently knew that he had been impotent for a long time and that he had waited at the pool for a long time. Notice His approach to him.

When Jesus saw him lie, and knew that he had been now a long time in that case, he saith unto him, Wilt thou be made whole? [John 5:6].

That's a peculiar question to ask a sick man. It seems rather absurd, doesn't it? Of course, he wanted to be made whole, but the Lord asked him the question for two reasons. First, to beget hope in the man. His case was hopeless, and I think the light of hope had pretty much gone out of his life, and he was in despair. Secondly, and this is the most important, Jesus wanted to get the man's eyes off the pool. Jesus wanted him to look to Him. I think this man had never noticed anybody else who came up there. He never watched anything else but just kept his eyes on the pool. So our Lord startled him with the question, "Do you earnestly desire to be made whole?" I think the man normally and naturally would look up. Who would ask a question like that? His answer was, "Of course, I want to be made whole. But that's not my problem. What I need is somebody to put me in the water."

The condition of so many people today is just like that man who was watching that pool, waiting for something to happen. I'm bold enough to say that it is the condition of all of us in these days. We are waiting. Just think of the people in our churches, waiting for some great, sweeping emotion to engulf them. Then there are those who are postponing making a decision for Christ. They are not willing to turn to Him because they are looking for an emotion; they are looking for something to happen. Another great group of people today have their eyes on business, and they are waiting for something to happen to get rich quick. I was pastor in Texas in a place where they drilled for oil, and I knew a lot of my folk who just sat around watching a dry well. There wasn't any moving of water or anything else. It was dry. They wanted that to become an oil well, and they had their eyes on the physical. Because they were entranced by the material, they lost sight of Jesus Christ. Then there are some people today who are looking to some individual. They've heard of the experience of someone else, and they are waiting for something like that to happen in their lives. But they are doomed to bitter disappointment. I've talked to many of these people. They come under all of these categories. They are all waiting with their eyes fixed on some *thing*. Unfortunately, they have their eyes fixed on the wrong thing, or the wrong individual, or the wrong happening. I'll ask you a question. Are you waiting for something to happen these days? If you tell me what it is, I could write your biography. The Thessalonians ". . . turned to God from idols to serve the living and true God" (1 Thess. 1:9). They took their eyes off things in Thessalonica, and they turned to the Lord Jesus Christ.

I'm sure this man looked up rather amazed that anyone would ask him that question.

The impotent man answered him, Sir, I have no man, when the water is troubled, to put me into the pool: but

> **while I am coming, another steppeth down before me**
> **[John 5:7].**

What a sad story that tells. This poor, helpless, hopeless, homeless, lonely fellow is really saying, "Would I be made whole? Of course, I would. But I haven't anybody to put me in the pool. Would You put me in the pool?" The Lord Jesus has no notion of getting that man into the pool. He is going to get him out of it and away from it. The minute the man gets his eye on the Lord Jesus, something will happen.

> **Jesus saith unto him, Rise, take up thy bed, and walk**
> **[John 5:8].**

He told him to rise (get up), take up his bed, and walk. He was to give up his place there at the pool to somebody else. He's to take his bed because no arrangements will be made for a relapse. There isn't going to be any relapse!

> **And immediately the man was made whole, and took**
> **up his bed, and walked: and on the same day was the**
> **sabbath.**
>
> **The Jews therefore said unto him that was cured, It is**
> **the sabbath day: it is not lawful for thee to carry thy bed.**
>
> **He answered them, He that made me whole, the same**
> **said unto me, Take up thy bed, and walk.**
>
> **Then asked they him, What man is that which said unto**
> **thee, Take up thy bed, and walk?**
>
> **And he that was healed wist not who it was: for Jesus**
> **had conveyed himself away, a multitude being in that**
> **place [John 5:9–13].**

The next thing that happens is that the enemies accuse the man of carrying his bed on the Sabbath Day. Well, that was the proof that he was healed. Can you imagine how ridiculous these religious rulers were to be upset because he carried his bed on the Sabbath Day?

Our Lord seemed to use a miraculous way of getting away from the crowd there that day because the man really didn't know who it was that had healed him.

Afterward Jesus findeth him in the temple, and said unto him, Behold, thou art made whole: sin no more, lest a worse thing come unto thee.

The man departed, and told the Jews that it was Jesus, which had made him whole.

And therefore did the Jews persecute Jesus, and sought to slay him, because he had done these things on the sabbath day [John 5:14–16].

What actually happened was simply this: the Lord healed him physically at the pool of Bethesda, but He healed his soul there in the temple. Sin had caused the man's trouble. First he got a well body, and then he got a well soul. He came to know Jesus, you see. Then he was able to tell who He was. This impotent man was waiting and waiting, looking at the pool, and one day Jesus, the Lamb of God, came by and saw him. Then the man saw Jesus. The impotent man met the Omnipotent Man. The thing that is amazing to me is that there were multitudes left in those porches and they were not healed. Today there are multitudes who are not saved. Isn't Jesus willing to save them? Yes, but they haven't looked at Jesus. They're just waiting, friend, waiting for something to happen.

This is the incident that put those bloodhounds of hate on the trail of Jesus. (When John says the "Jews," he is actually referring to the religious rulers of the Jews.) This is the point at which they began to persecute Jesus and sought to slay Him.

But Jesus answered them, My Father worketh hitherto, and I work [John 5:17].

When that man got down into the ditch of sin, the Lord Jesus and the Father could no longer rest on the Sabbath Day. Although God rested after the creation of the physical universe, after the fall of man He didn't rest, because man, like an ox, had gotten down into the ditch.

> **Therefore the Jews sought the more to kill him, because he not only had broken the sabbath, but said also that God was his Father, making himself equal with God [John 5:18].**

These men never let up until they folded their arms beneath His cross.

THE CLAIMS OF JESUS

Our Lord now goes on to make three tremendous claims concerning Himself. It is on the basis of these claims that we can use John 5:24 in presenting the gospel. We will try to put it all together here.

The first claim:

> **Then answered Jesus and said unto them, Verily, verily, I say unto you, The Son can do nothing of himself, but what he seeth the Father do: for what things soever he doeth, these also doeth the Son likewise [John 5:19].**

The Lord Jesus is saying that He is God and that He can do what God does. There is a perfect correspondence and harmony between the Father and the Son. Therefore, the charge that was made against Him was absurd. The Son does not contradict the Father, nor does the Father contradict the Son. Jesus does what God does. Jesus can forgive sins. Then He goes on to say that there is a personal and intimate relationship between the Father and the Son.

> **For the Father loveth the Son, and sheweth him all things that himself doeth: and he will shew him greater works than these, that ye may marvel [John 5:20].**

The second claim:

For as the Father raiseth up the dead, and quickeneth them; even so the Son quickeneth whom he will [John 5:21].

Jesus imparts life, gives life, to whom He will. If the Father raises the dead, the Son will raise the dead. Today we hear a great deal being said about the gift of healing, but with that gift went the ability to raise the dead. Paul raised the dead, and so did Simon Peter. Our Lord gave them that gift. It was an apostolic gift of healing and raising the dead, which disappeared with the apostles. The Lord Jesus raised the dead. He raised the dead because He was God. These other men did it in the name of the Lord Jesus.

The third claim:

For the Father judgeth no man, but hath committed all judgment unto the Son [John 5:22].

A literal reading would be, "For not even the Father judgeth anyone, but He hath given all judgment unto the Son." You can have everlasting life if you hear His word and believe it. Why? Because the Lord Jesus does what God does, because He raises the dead, and because He is going to judge all men someday. Whether saved or lost, they are going to appear before Him. The believers will appear before Him at the judgment which we call the Bema seat of Christ to see whether they receive a reward (see 2 Cor. 5:10). The lost will come before Him at the Great White Throne (see Rev. 20:11). Remember that the Lord Jesus did not come to judge the first time, but He will come as Judge the next time, and *all* judgment is committed to Him.

Jesus definitely puts Himself on a par with God the Father.

That all men should honour the Son, even as they honour the Father. He that honoureth not the Son honoureth not the Father which hath sent him [John 5:23].

It is on the basis of these three claims, these three great principles, that He goes on to this wonderful statement in verse 24 which is used so much in personal work today. It is right that we should use it, but we need to remember to back it up with these claims Jesus has just made.

> **Verily, verily, I say unto you, He that heareth my word, and believeth on him that sent me, hath everlasting life, and shall not come into condemnation; but is passed from death unto life [John 5:24].**

Notice that He says, "*hath* everlasting life," which is right now—present tense. The believer does not come into *condemnation,* which is another word for judgment. He is passed out of death into life.

Now who is saying this? This is a tremendous promise, but who is making it? That is the important thing.

Years ago, in a cotton patch in my southland, a man stood up and read to those that were weary from picking cotton and were lying on their sacks. He read, "Come unto me, all ye that labour and are heavy laden, and I will give you rest" (Matt. 11:28). One man raised himself from off his cotton sack and said, "Them's good words, but who said them?"

Well, these are good words: "He that heareth my word, and believeth on him that sent me, hath everlasting life, and shall not come into condemnation; but is passed from death unto life." Who said them? Christ has given us the three statements concerning Himself which are the foundation for this verse. Jesus is God (v. 19); He raises the dead (v. 21); and He is going to judge (v. 22). Who He is makes these words truly wonderful words.

Now Jesus goes on with another great statement.

> **Verily, verily, I say unto you, The hour is coming, and now is, when the dead shall hear the voice of the Son of God: and they that hear shall live.**

> **Marvel not at this: for the hour is coming, in the which all that are in the graves shall hear his voice [John 5:25, 28].**

What does He mean in verse 25 when He says, "the hour . . . now is"? Well, we're in that period of the hour that is coming. Verse 28 makes it clear that the hour has not yet arrived, but "the hour is coming." The whole thought is that we are living in the period or the age or the dispensation that is moving to the time when "the dead shall hear the voice of the Son of God: and they that hear shall live."

If we are in the period of the "hour that is coming," then what does He mean that it also "now is"? Who are the dead who hear His voice now? In John 11 where we have the incident in which Jesus raised Lazarus from the dead, you will remember that He said to the two sisters at the time of the death of Lazarus, "I am the resurrection, and the life: he that believeth in me, *though he were dead,* yet shall he live: and whosoever liveth and believeth in me shall never die" (John 11:25–26, italics mine). "Though he were dead." Does this mean the person that is in the grave hears? No, no, this is referring to spiritual death! Death means separation from God. The hour *is coming* when those who are in the grave shall hear His voice and shall live, but the hour *is now* when those who are spiritually dead hear His voice and live. Paul wrote to the Ephesian believers that they had been dead in trespasses and sins. That is the spiritual condition of everyone. But then, "he that heareth my word, and believeth on him that sent me, hath everlasting life, and shall not come into condemnation; but is passed from death [out of spiritual death] unto life," the life that He gives. So in verses 25 and 28 He is talking about two separate things. The time is now when Christ gives spiritual life. The hour is coming when He will raise the dead out of the grave.

For as the Father hath life in himself; so hath he given to the Son to have life in himself;

And hath given him authority to execute judgment also, because he is the Son of man [John 5:26–27].

The Lord Jesus is a life-giver, you see. Not only does He have life, but He gives life. He also has the right to execute judgment. He came the first time as the Savior and not to judge, but He is coming the next time as the Judge. At that time, those in the graves will hear His voice.

> **Marvel not at this: for the hour is coming, in the which all that are in the graves shall hear his voice,**

> **And shall come forth; they that have done good, unto the resurrection of life; and they that have done evil, unto the resurrection of damnation [John 5:28–29].**

A better translation for the word *damnation* would be "judgment."

There are two resurrections mentioned here. The Book of Revelation is even more specific and describes the completion of the first resurrection (Rev. 20:4–6) and the second resurrection (Rev. 20:11–15). The first resurrection is the resurrection of all the saved—the first phase of which is the next thing on the agenda of God. We call it the rapture of the church. "Rapture" is a good translation of the Greek *harpazō*. Paul used it in 1 Thessalonians 4:17 where he says we shall be "caught up," which means "to be raptured." The Rapture takes place at some time in the future. It is not dated and there are no signs given for it. It could happen at any moment. He is going to call His own out of this world, both the living and the dead. That is part of the first resurrection. Then, during the Tribulation period a great many believers will become martyrs. They will be raised at the end of the Great Tribulation period together with the Old Testament saints. That also is part of the first resurrection. They will be raised to live forever here upon this earth. That is the first resurrection. It is the resurrection of life, as our Lord called it.

Then the resurrection of judgment is the Great White Throne judgment when all the unsaved of all the ages will be raised. They wanted to be judged by their works, and they will be! They will stand before God who is just and righteous; they will have an opportunity to stand before a Holy God and to plead their case. But God has already warned them; there is no one saved in that judgment. It is only the lost who are brought there, and they will be judged according to their works, because there are degrees in punishment (see Luke 12:47–48).

> **I can of mine own self do nothing: as I hear, I judge: and my judgment is just; because I seek not mine own will, but the will of the Father which hath sent me [John 5:30].**

Jesus says, "I can of mine own self do nothing." That is His self-limitation when He came down to this earth and took upon Himself our humanity. He came down as a man, not to do His own will but the Father's will.

This is the example for us today. You and I have a will, an old nature, that is not obedient to God. We can't be obedient to God because we are actually in rebellion against God. That is the natural state of every man. That is the reason our Lord had to tell Nicodemus that he must be born again. Those who are in the flesh cannot please God. "That which is born of the flesh is flesh; and that which is born of the Spirit is spirit" (John 3:6). You and I have to have the new birth because this old nature is incorrigible, my friend. It is in rebellion against God. It has been carrying a protest banner before the gates of heaven ever since man came out through the gates of paradise in the Garden of Eden.

Now our Lord is going to show that there are witnesses to the fact that His claims are true.

If I bear witness of myself, my witness is not true.

There is another that beareth witness of me; and I know that the witness which he witnesseth of me is true [John 5:31–32].

The Scripture teaches that in the mouth of two or three witnesses a thing is established. "I bear witness of myself"—that would not stand up in court. But, "There is another that beareth witness of me." The witness He is referring to here is not John the Baptist. They would immediately think that is the one to whom He is referring, but He makes it clear that He is not referring to a human witness at all.

Ye sent unto John, and he bare witness unto the truth [John 5:33].

Now, He is saying that John the Baptist did bare witness to Him. So that is one witness whom they knew. But He is referring to still an-

other Witness, not a human witness, and that makes two witnesses for
them to recognize.

> **But I receive not testimony from man: but these things I
> say, that ye might be saved [John 5:34].**

He claims a higher Witness than the witness of man. Yet, He does give
a testimony to John the Baptist. In our King James Version He calls
John a "light." A more accurate translation is "lamp." You see, Jesus is
the Light; John was His witness, His light bearer, His lamp, if you
please.

> **He was a burning and a shining light: and ye were will-
> ing for a season to rejoice in his light.**

> **But I have greater witness than that of John: for the
> works which the Father hath given me to finish, the
> same works that I do, bear witness of me, that the Father
> hath sent me [John 5:35–36].**

Here we see that the credentials that the Lord Jesus had were the miracles that He performed. This idea today that there are those who have
the same power that Jesus had is, to my judgment, blasphemy. You
see, these miracles which He performed attested that He was who He
claimed to be. And, friend, there weren't just a few isolated instances
of healing. He didn't put on healing services. He took no offerings. He
didn't have people get in a line and come by Him. He moved out into
the crowds, into the highways and the byways. And as He moved
along, people were healed. I've called attention to this in the Gospels
again and again, and it is important to refresh our memories concerning this. Friend, there were not just a half dozen, or even a hundred or
two whom He had healed; there were literally thousands of people
whom He had healed. It was openly demonstrated. Nobody in that day
contradicted the fact that He healed—he would have been a fool if he
had. It is over nineteen hundred years later in a musty library in New
York City, thousands of miles removed, that scholars can sit down and

write books declaring that they don't believe Jesus performed miracles. But that doesn't prove a thing, friend. His miracles were His credentials. His works bore witness that the Father had sent Him.

> **And the Father himself, which hath sent me, hath borne witness of me. Ye have neither heard his voice at any time, nor seen his shape.**

> **And ye have not his word abiding in you: for whom he hath sent, him ye believe not.**

> **Search the scriptures; for in them ye think ye have eternal life: and they are they which testify of me [John 5:37–39].**

This last verse is so frequently misunderstood. It is not an imperative but is an indicative. Let me put it like this: "You search the Scriptures." He's making a statement; He is not urging them to do something. He tells them that they search the Scriptures thinking that in them they will find eternal life, but they don't understand that the Scriptures testify of Jesus. Friend, you had better be careful so that you find Jesus in the Bible. If you don't, then your search is in vain.

> **And ye will not come to me, that ye might have life [John 5:40].**

The Scriptures speak of Him, but the religious rulers are unwilling to come to Him. They are missing the point.

> **But I know you, that ye have not the love of God in you.**

> **I am come in my Father's name, and ye receive me not: if another shall come in his own name, him ye will receive [John 5:42–43].**

Someday the Antichrist is coming, and the world will receive him. They rejected Christ. The Antichrist will come in his own name, will have an image made of himself, and they will accept him.

> **How can ye believe, which receive honour one of another, and seek not the honour that cometh from God only? [John 5:44].**

They looked for the applause of men. Back scratching is still the curse today in our churches, even our good churches. There are teachers with itching ears. Each one wants to compliment the other rather than tell the truth of the Word of God. They "seek not the honour that cometh from God only."

> **Do not think that I will accuse you to the Father: there is one that accuseth you, even Moses, in whom ye trust.**
>
> **For had ye believed Moses, ye would have believed me: for he wrote of me.**
>
> **But if ye believe not his writings, how shall ye believe my words? [John 5:45–47].**

Friend, that is so important. Back in the books of the Pentateuch which I have recently taught, I have attempted to point out the Lord Jesus. Although I don't find Him on every page, I believe He *is* on every page of the Pentateuch. He says, "Moses . . . wrote of me." I think He is on every page of the Bible.

When a man begins to make an attack upon the Old Testament, watch out! He really is making a subtle attack on the Lord Jesus Christ. I'm afraid there are many men who very foolishly begin to question the Old Testament and don't realize what they are doing. It is like the man at the insane asylum who was digging at the foundation. A man came by and asked, "Why are you trying to dig out the foundation? Don't you live in the building?" "Yes," he answered, "but I live upstairs!" I'm afraid that a great many foolish people say, "But I live in the New Testament." My friend, the Old Testament is the foundation. Our Lord said, "If you believe not his writings, how shall you believe my words?" They both go together.

CHAPTER 6

THEME: *Jesus feeds five thousand near Sea of Galilee (fourth work and word)*

We come now to the miraculous feeding of the five thousand—a miracle recorded in all four Gospels. In the Gospel of John, Jesus follows this miracle with a discourse on the Bread of Life. John records only certain miracles, and he calls the miracles *signs* because signs are for a purpose. You will remember that he said, "And many other signs truly did Jesus in the presence of his disciples, which are not written in this book: But these are written, that ye might believe that Jesus is the Christ, the Son of God; and that believing ye might have life through his name" (John 20:30–31). This is an important verse because it is actually the key to this entire Gospel.

Now we find Jesus feeding the five thousand, and out of this grows His great discourse on the fact that He is the true Bread of God.

JESUS FEEDS THE FIVE THOUSAND
(Fourth Work and Word)

After these things Jesus went over the sea of Galilee, which is the sea of Tiberias [John 6:1].

After what things? Well, the things that were recorded back in the fifth chapter. He had left Jerusalem and probably had come up on the east side of the Jordan River. Now He crosses over the Sea of Galilee and, apparently, comes to the north section. This took place about six months to a year after the events of chapter 5. It was about one year before His crucifixion, by the way.

The way the events are dated is by the feasts that John mentions. As we have said, John ties his Gospel down to a calendar and to a map. The One who came out of heaven's glory, the Word who was made flesh, the One who pitched His tent here among us, that One walked by the Sea of Galilee, went to Cana and to Nazareth, Capernaum, Bethsaida, Jerusalem, Decapolis, etc. So we read that "after these things Jesus went over the sea of Galilee." John says, "And the passover, a feast of the Jews, was nigh" (v. 4). So apparently He had been back in the land of Galilee, because in chapter 5 He had been in Jerusalem and had gone in the sheep gate. This indicates a time lapse between chapters 5 and 6 when He went over the Sea of Galilee.

And a great multitude followed him, because they saw his miracles which he did on them that were diseased [John 6:2].

The tense of the verb would be more accurate if it were translated, "And a great multitude was following Him" and "because they were seeing His miracles."

This great multitude didn't actually believe in Him in a saving way. They didn't trust Him. They were interested in His miracles. They wanted Him because He could make them well.

Friend, the mission of Jesus was not to restore our physical bodies. He wants to be Lord of our hearts. This is why John had said at the very beginning that He "needed not that any should testify of man; for he knew what was in man" (John 2:25). He didn't commit Himself to that crowd back there at Jerusalem, and He's not about to commit Himself to this crowd that is gathering around now. They simply want to see the miracles that He can perform.

And Jesus went up into a mountain, and there he sat with his disciples [John 6:3].

The place that is pointed out to tourists visiting Israel is not what we would call a mountain. Actually, in that land three thousand feet is about as high as they go, but the hills are very rugged. The one they point out is a very lovely spot and could well be the place where He fed the five thousand. It's near Capernaum, by the way.

Jesus went up into the mountain and sat there with His disciples. The Passover was near.

When Jesus then lifted up his eyes, and saw a great company come unto him, he saith unto Philip, Whence shall we buy bread, that these may eat? [John 6:5].

Philip was the quiet one; he never had much to say. Our Lord was drawing him out at this particular time. You will find in verse 8 that Philip and Andrew seem to have gotten together. Andrew and Philip evidently were quite active men, very busy, but just not speakers. You don't hear either one of them. Yet Andrew is the one who brought Simon Peter to the Lord, and the Greeks came to Philip and Andrew when they wanted to see Jesus. Philip got together with Andrew to find out what to do. So we find them together here.

Is our Lord asking for advice in His question to Philip? May I say to you, He never asked for advice. Then why did He ask Philip the question?

And this he said to prove him: for he himself knew what he would do [John 6:6].

He was testing Philip. Philip looked over that crowd that was coming—five thousand men besides women and children. I estimate it must have been at least fifteen thousand people. Friend, that's a pretty good–sized crowd, especially for that land and in that day. When Philip saw them coming, he wasn't thinking of a miracle at all.

Philip answered him, Two hundred pennyworth of bread is not sufficient for them, that every one of them may take a little [John 6:7].

Why did Philip light upon that fixed sum of two hundred denarii? I think that is what they had in the treasury at that time. Probably Judas had made a treasurer's report that morning, and that was the total. Philip looked at the crowd, then thought of what they had in the treasury bag, and said that two hundred pennyworth of bread would not be sufficient for them. The "penny" was the Roman coin *denarius*. One denarius represented a day's wages for a common laborer.

The other Gospel writers tell us that the disciples advised the Lord Jesus. They wanted to be on the board of directors. They said, "Why don't You send the multitude away?" Our Lord answered, "We're not going to send them away. We're going to have them sit down and we're going to feed them" (cf. Luke 9:12–15). These men who had elected themselves to the board of directors found themselves waiters, serving the crowd. And that is what they should have been doing all the time.

By the way, this leads me to say that there are too many men in the church today who want position. They want to have an office; they want to be on the board of directors. They like to tell the preacher what to do. Yet they do not have all the necessary information to begin with, nor do they have spiritual discernment. They don't realize that they are the ones who ought to be out doing the work of the ministry. They ought to be out witnessing for the Lord—passing the bread to the hungry multitudes. But generally they would rather advise the pastor how to do it.

So here our Lord is drawing out Philip, and Philip says they don't have enough money to buy sufficient bread. Since Philip and Andrew are together, Andrew speaks up.

There is a lad here, which hath five barley loaves, and two small fishes: but what are they among so many? [John 6:9].

Andrew, you see, had been circulating around through the crowd, making a survey. Surveys are important, I guess, but they are seldom very helpful. You can see Andrew and Philip there together. Philip says the money in the treasury won't feed them. Andrew says all he's found is a little lad with five barley loaves and two small fish. Remember, these five barley loaves were not big commercial loaves of bread or family loaves. They were more like a hamburger bun. They were just big enough to put with the fish. That's all this man Andrew could produce. It was a hopeless project—"What are they among so many?"

And Jesus said, Make the men sit down. Now there was much grass in the place. So the men sat down, in number about five thousand [John 6:10].

I would call your attention to the fact that there were five thousand men. I think a woman and one child with each man would be a reasonable estimate of the crowd, which would be fifteen thousand people. Now the Lord Jesus is going to feed that multitude. Here is something, I think, that is interesting to note. If you have fifteen thousand people to feed, that is certainly a liability. If you have five loaves and two fish and also the two hundred denarii, then, friend, these are your total assets. May I say that if a committee would have handed in a report with those assets and those liabilities, they would have said, "There's nothing you can do about it." Someone has called a committee a group of people who individually can do nothing, and collectively they can decide that nothing can be done. Or, a committee is a group of people who take down minutes and waste hours. So here is the committee report: to feed them would be impossible.

You see, what you need in this equation is what I call the mathematics of a miracle. You need Jesus. I tell you, if you have the five loaves plus the two fishes plus Jesus, then you've got something, friend. Without Him, you don't have anything at all.

Jesus told them to make the men sit down, and they sat down. Mark emphasizes the fact that they sat down by companies; that is, each of the groups of people which had come from a certain section sat down together. They may have been distinguished by robes of a certain color from their area. Everything that our Lord did was done decently and in order. Each little group was color on the background of green grass. I am of the opinion that if you could have been on the hill on the opposite side from where these people were sitting, you would have seen something that would have been as beautiful as a patchwork quilt. It would have been very orderly, because our Lord was doing it.

And Jesus took the loaves; and when he had given thanks, he distributed to the disciples, and the disciples

> to them that were set down; and likewise of the fishes as
> much as they would.
>
> When they were filled, he said unto his disciples,
> Gather up the fragments that remain, that nothing be
> lost.
>
> Therefore they gathered them together, and filled twelve
> baskets with the fragments of the five barley loaves,
> which remained over and above unto them that had
> eaten [John 6:11–13].

As a student in a liberal college, I never shall forget how the professor explained away this miracle. What he said was that the disciples had gathered together these loaves and fishes ahead of time and had stored them up in a cave. Then the Lord Jesus just backed up to that cave, and the disciples just sort of slipped them out under His arm, concealed by a flowing robe! It was sort of like hocus-pocus, abracadabra. The only thing wrong with that explanation is that it won't work. You would have to have more faith to believe *that* than to believe it just like it is, my friend. To begin with, where would they find a bakery in that area that could provide that many loaves? And where would they get that many fish for this particular occasion at this time? We have no record that Andrew and Peter had been out fishing! This explanation is utterly preposterous and ridiculous, as you can see.

The obvious explanation is that a miracle was performed here. When you add Jesus to the side of the assets, you have more than enough. In fact, you have twelve baskets of leftovers. That doesn't mean they were scraps. I used to think that a fellow would bite on a sandwich, then when he would see a bigger one, he would put the first one down and reach over and get the new sandwich so that the fragments were that which had been partially eaten. That's not true. There were twelve baskets of sandwiches that weren't even touched, my friend. Do you know what this means? It means that the crowd got all they wanted to eat. And people in that land and in that day were often hungry. There were many people in the crowd there that day who for the first time in their lives had their tummies filled. You see, when the Lord Jesus does anything, He does a good job of it.

> **Then those men, when they had seen the miracle that Jesus did, said, This is of a truth that prophet that should come into the world.**
>
> **When Jesus therefore perceived that they would come and take him by force, to make him a king, he departed again into a mountain himself alone [John 6:14–15].**

You see, they are following Him because He's a miracle worker. And I'm almost sure that He had to perform another miracle to get free from the crowd. The reason He got free from them was because they wanted to make Him a king. "Well," someone says, "isn't He a King?" Yes, it is true that He was born a King. But this is not the route by which He is coming to kingship.

JESUS WALKS ON THE WATER

> **And when even was now come, his disciples went down unto the sea,**
>
> **And entered into a ship, and went over the sea toward Capernaum. And it was now dark, and Jesus was not come to them.**
>
> **And the sea arose by reason of a great wind that blew.**
>
> **So when they had rowed about five and twenty or thirty furlongs, they see Jesus walking on the sea, and drawing nigh unto the ship: and they were afraid.**
>
> **But he saith unto them, It is I; be not afraid.**
>
> **Then they willingly received him into the ship: and immediately the ship was at the land whither they went [John 6:16–21].**

The other Gospels tell us that He hurried the disciples down to the Sea of Galilee and put them on a boat to go across while He went up into the mountain to pray. Since those mountains are about three thousand feet high, a storm from them will break suddenly upon the Sea of Galilee—and this was a real storm! When they were twenty-five or thirty furlongs out on the sea, they were halfway across. It was in the middle of this inland sea that they saw Jesus walking on the water. They were afraid because they didn't recognize Him.

The same liberal professor who explained away the feeding of the five thousand tried to explain away this miracle too. He said the ship was at the land, so Jesus was actually walking on the shore—but the disciples *thought* that He was walking on the water. May I say that John had been a fisherman on this Sea of Galilee, and he knew it well. He specifically mentions their position in the lake so we would know they were not at the shore.

Jesus came to them in the storm. And that is a time He comes to His own today. He makes Himself more real to us in a time of trouble and sorrow. I don't know why He waits until midnight, until the waves are rolling, but perhaps that is the only time we will listen to Him. When the storms of life are beating upon our little bark, our hearts are ready for His presence.

"Immediately the ship was at the land whither they went." This may be another miracle, or John may mean that with no delay they reached the other side since the water was now calm. Or it may be the language of love—with Him in the boat it didn't seem far to the other side.

JESUS GIVES A DISCOURSE ON THE
BREAD OF LIFE

We find now that the crowd is beginning to look for Him, and they are disappointed. They discover that both the Lord Jesus and the disciples are gone.

The day following, when the people which stood on the other side of the sea saw that there was none other boat

there, save that one whereinto his disciples were entered, and that Jesus went not with his disciples into the
boat, but that his disciples were gone away alone;

(Howbeit there came other boats from Tiberias nigh
unto the place where they did eat bread, after that the
Lord had given thanks:)

When the people therefore saw that Jesus was not there,
neither his disciples, they also took shipping, and came
to Capernaum, seeking for Jesus [John 6:22–24].

They apparently had come up from the southern part of the Sea of
Galilee, and He had fed them there. Then they had come on by boat to
Capernaum. That seems to be the way we have it here.

This is the first time John used the title Lord—"After that the Lord
had given thanks." As we have seen, the common name John uses for
Him is Jesus because He is "the Word . . . made flesh" (John 1:14).
Who is that Word? It is Jesus. ". . . thou shalt call his name JESUS: for
he shall save his people from their sins" (Matt. 1:21).

The crowd was really wanting to know how He had been able to
get away as He did.

And when they had found him on the other side of the
sea, they said unto him, Rabbi, when camest thou
hither?

Jesus answered them and said, Verily, verily, I say unto
you, Ye seek me, not because ye saw the miracles, but
because ye did eat of the loaves, and were filled [John
6:25–26].

Jesus doesn't really answer their question directly. He penetrated beneath the surface to their motive for seeking Him. Actually, the word
He used was not literally "loaves" but a word that means fodder. You
ate the fodder and were filled. Your only interest was that your tummies were full.

> **Labour not for the meat which perisheth, but for that meat which endureth unto everlasting life, which the Son of man shall give unto you: for him hath God the Father sealed [John 6:27].**

Let me put this into our language of today (this is not a translation but only an attempt to bring out the meaning): stop working for food that perishes, but work for food that endures for everlasting life, which food the Son of Man will give you, for on Him, God the Father has set His seal.

You will recall that this is the same approach which our Lord made to the woman at the well. For her it was water that she wanted; for these folk it is bread. These are two essential things. Bread and water are very important to maintain life. Jesus is both Bread and Water. Notice that He uses these commonplace symbols. He is the Word, and the Word became flesh. How can we explain that? Jesus, the Word, is reaching down and communicating where we can understand it. He said that He is Water and that He gives Living Water. He said that He is Bread. We know what water is and we know what bread is.

> **Then said they unto him, What shall we do, that we might work the works of God? [John 6:28].**

In other words, they are asking what they can *do* to be saved. Man has always felt that if he could just work at it, he could be saved. Man feels thoroughly capable of working out his own salvation. He feels competent to do it, and he feels that God must accept his works. Notice carefully what the work of God is.

> **Jesus answered and said unto them, This is the work of God, that ye believe on him whom he hath sent [John 6:29].**

You see, the work of God is not that which is commanded by God, but it is that which has been wrought by God. In other words, it is what God has done and not what you do. It is the work of God and not the works of man. "This is the work of God, that ye *believe* on him whom he hath sent." He is saying that God provided food. He is the One who has provided that for us today, and we are to partake of it. The invitation He gives is to a banquet. Go out on the byways and highways and tell them they are invited to come. It is a free meal, by the way, but it happens to be spiritual food.

> **They said therefore unto him, What sign shewest thou then, that we may see, and believe thee? what dost thou work? [John 6:30].**

May I say that this reveals the hardness of the human heart. Here are the men who had been fed miraculously by our Lord when He fed the five thousand and they say, "Show us a sign. What dost Thou work?" In other words, they did not want to believe at all. And they take their conversation right back to the dinner table.

> **Our fathers did eat manna in the desert; as it is written, He gave them bread from heaven to eat.**
>
> **Then Jesus said unto them, Verily, verily, I say unto you, Moses gave you not that bread from heaven; but my Father giveth you the true bread from heaven.**
>
> **For the bread of God is he which cometh down from heaven, and giveth life unto the world [John 6:31–33].**

They are still thinking of physical food, and say, "Moses gave our people manna." Actually it wasn't Moses who gave the manna; God did that. And it wasn't a one-time deal. God fed them every day for forty years. They want to be fed, and that is what they are after. Manna gave life in that day, and it was a gift from God. The manna gave physical life to them out there in the wilderness, but the Lord Jesus gives spiritual life. "My Father giveth you the true bread from heaven."

> **Then said they unto him, Lord, evermore give us this bread [John 6:34].**

They are just like the woman at the well who asked for water but was thinking of physical water so she wouldn't need to come and draw water at the well anymore. It took our Lord quite a while to lift her thinking out of that well to the spiritual Water. And it takes Him a long time to get these folk away from the dinner table and get them to see the spiritual Bread that gives spiritual life.

> **And Jesus said unto them, I am the bread of life: he that cometh to me shall never hunger; and he that believeth on me shall never thirst [John 6:35].**

He joins the two together. Christ is the manna. He is the One who came down from heaven and gave His life for the world that we might have life. That is salvation. We will also see that He is the Bread that we are to feed upon constantly so that we might grow spiritually. After all, manna was miracle food, and it was thrilling. When the children of Israel got into the Promised Land, they were given the "old corn of the land" which symbolizes the Word of God. Believe me, lots of people don't like the "old corn."

> **But I said unto you, That ye also have seen me, and believe not.**

> **All that the Father giveth me shall come to me; and him that cometh to me I will in no wise cast out [John 6:36–37].**

"You want bread? Well, I am the Bread of Life. But you have seen Me, and you do not believe. All that the Father gives Me shall come to Me; and him that comes to Me I will in no wise cast out."

This thirty-seventh verse is a very important verse. There is a theological argument that rages today on election or free will. There are some people who put all their eggs in the basket of election. There are others who put all their eggs in the basket of free will. I'm not proposing to reconcile the two because I have discovered that I cannot. If you had met me the year that I entered seminary, or the year I graduated, I could have reconciled them for you. I never have been as smart as I was my first year and my last year in seminary. I knew it all then. I could reconcile election and free will, and it was a marvelous explanation. Now I've even forgotten what it was. It was pretty silly, if you want to know the truth.

Election and free will are both in this verse. "All that the father giveth me shall come to me" states a truth, and that is election. But wait a minute! "And him that cometh to me I will in no wise cast out" is also true, and "him that cometh to me" is free will. I don't know how to reconcile them, but they are both true. The Father gives men to Christ, but men have to come. And the ones that come are the ones, apparently, whom the Father gives to Him. You and I are down here, and we don't see into the machinery of heaven. I don't know how God runs that computer of election, but I know that He has given to you and to me a free will and we have to exercise it.

Because Spurgeon preached a "whosoever will" gospel, someone said to him, "If I believed like you do about election, I wouldn't preach like you do." Spurgeon's answer was something like this, "If the Lord had put a yellow stripe down the backs of the elect, I'd go up and down the street lifting up shirttails, finding out who had the yellow stripe, and then I'd give them the gospel. But God didn't do it that way. He told me to preach the gospel to every creature that 'whosoever will may come.'" Jesus says, ". . . and him that cometh to me I will in no wise cast out." So, my friend, you can argue about election all you want to, but you can come. And if you come, He'll not cast you out.

Someone may ask, "You mean that if I'm not the elect I can still come?" My friend, if you come, you will be the elect. How tremendous this is!

For I came down from heaven, not to do mine own will, but the will of him that sent me [John 6:38].

How wonderful it is that the *will* of God is for you to come to Him. Jesus came down from heaven because "the Son of man must be lifted up." He came to do the Father's will in that, and it is the Father's will that you be born again. But you will have to come to Him, friend; that is the only way. You must come to the Lord Jesus by faith.

> **And this is the Father's will which hath sent me, that of all which he hath given me I should lose nothing, but should raise it up again at the last day [John 6:39].**

The term *predestination* applies only to the saved. It means just exactly what He is saying here. When a person accepts Christ, he is justified; and just as surely as he is justified, he is going to be glorified. When Jesus starts out with one hundred sheep, He's going to come through with one hundred sheep. He will not lose one. That is what this means. Everyone who believes and receives Christ has everlasting life and will be raised up again at the last day.

> **The Jews then murmured at him, because he said, I am the bread which came down from heaven.**
>
> **And they said, Is not this Jesus, the son of Joseph, whose father and mother we know? how is it then that he saith, I came down from heaven? [John 6:41-42].**

You see, He taught that He was God and that He came down from heaven. May I say to you, in this section here He is teaching His virgin birth. There are those who say the Lord Jesus never taught that He was virgin born. What do you think He is saying here, friend? The Jews understood what He was saying. They asked how this could be when they knew His father and His mother. Well, it's by the virgin birth. As the angel told Mary, it was the Holy Spirit who conceived that "holy thing" in Mary (see Luke 1:35). This section right here (beginning with v. 38) is a complement or a counterpart of the virgin birth and needs to be added to the other portions of Scripture which deal with it. "I came down from heaven"—that's the Christmas story. "Out of the ivory palaces into a world of woe." He came down from heaven's glory; He stepped down from the throne to ascend the Cross for you and for me. He did it by way of the virgin birth. You can have the jingle of bells and all the Ho, Ho, Hos—but that is not Christmas. The virgin birth of the Lord Jesus Christ is the Christmas story.

They got the message immediately and asked, "Is not this Jesus, the son of Joseph?" They thought they knew His father and His mother, but He is not the son of Joseph. He came down from heaven.

> **Jesus therefore answered and said unto them, Murmur not among yourselves.**
>
> **No man can come to me, except the Father which hath sent me draw him: and I will raise him up at the last day [John 6:43–44].**

Actually, the word translated "draw" is *drag*. That is divine election. You ask me to explain it? I can't explain it at all, friend; I just know that you have a free will, and you can exercise it. God holds you responsible for it, and you know you are responsible. You know right now you can come or not come. It's up to you.

> **It is written in the prophets, And they shall be all taught of God. Every man therefore that hath heard, and hath learned of the Father, cometh unto me [John 6:45].**

There is Scripture after Scripture in the Old Testament that refers to this. For instance, Isaiah 54:13: "And all thy children shall be taught of the LORD; and great shall be the peace of thy children." Isaiah 60:2–3: "For, behold, the darkness shall cover the earth, and gross darkness the people: but the LORD shall arise upon thee, and his glory shall be seen upon thee. And the Gentiles shall come to thy light, and kings to the brightness of thy rising." There are these statements that they will come to Him, and you can come to Him. These things are made so wonderfully clear. There are many references to it. Malachi 4:2 is another: "But unto you that fear my name shall the Sun of righteousness arise with healing in his wings; and ye shall to forth, and grow up as calves of the stall." Every man that listens to the Father and learns of Him will come to Me is what He is saying. You see, if you

listen to the Word of God, then you'll come to Christ. That is where the
great emphasis is being placed here.

> **Not that any man hath seen the Father, save he which is
> of God, he hath seen the Father.**

> **Verily, verily, I say unto you, He that believeth on me
> hath everlasting life [John 6:46–47].**

The One who has seen the Father is the Lord Jesus Christ. "He who
believes on Me has everlasting life." It can't be said any more clearly.

> **I am that bread of life.**

> **Your fathers did eat manna in the wilderness, and are
> dead.**

> **This is the bread which cometh down from heaven, that
> a man may eat thereof, and not die.**

> **I am the living bread which came down from heaven: if
> any man eat of this bread, he shall live for ever: and the
> bread that I will give is my flesh, which I will give for
> the life of the world [John 6:48–51].**

He came down to this earth: "the Word was made flesh" (John 1:14).
He is going to the Cross to lay that human life down there as a sacrifice
to pay for your sins and my sins. Friend, when you partake of that,
that is, when you *accept* that, you are saved. Someone may say, "Oh,
that's so vivid and so strong." That's what they said in that day, too.

> **The Jews therefore strove among themselves, saying,
> How can this man give us his flesh to eat? [John 6:52].**

They were thinking of His literal flesh, of course.

> **Then Jesus said unto them, Verily, verily, I say unto you,
> Except ye eat the flesh of the Son of man, and drink his
> blood, ye have no life in you [John 6:53].**

That means to partake of Him spiritually, which is more real than a physical partaking.

> Whoso eateth my flesh, and drinketh my blood, hath eternal life; and I will raise him up at the last day.
>
> For my flesh is meat indeed, and my blood is drink indeed.
>
> He that eateth my flesh, and drinketh my blood, dwelleth in me, and I in him.
>
> As the living Father hath sent me, and I live by the father: so he that eateth me, even he shall live by me.
>
> This is that bread which came down from heaven: not as your fathers did eat manna, and are dead: he that eateth of this bread shall live for ever [John 6:54–58].

Friend, this is an amazing statement. Our Lord is preparing these men for that Last Supper and the institution of the Lord's Supper. This, obviously, is something that is not to be taken literally because He was right there before them. He is not saying for them to begin to eat Him and to drink His blood! What He is saying is that He is going to give His life. In that Upper Room He made it very clear that the blood is the symbol of life. "For the life of the flesh is in the blood . . . (Lev. 17:11). God had taught the Israelites that truth from the very beginning when He called them out of the land of Egypt. There at Mount Sinai Moses gives them this great axiom, "the life of the flesh is in the blood," which is also medically true, by the way. The life of the flesh *is* in the blood. And Jesus is giving His life. He will shed His blood upon the Cross and give His life. Salvation is by accepting and receiving Him in a most intimate way.

This is the basis for the sacrament of the Lord's Supper. Friend, there has been just as much disagreement among believers in the churches down through the ages over the interpretation of the Lord's Supper as there has been over baptism. I don't think they have fought over it quite as much, but the disagreement is there.

Hoc est meus corpus—"This is my body." When He gave them the bread at the supper in the Upper Room, He said, ". . . This is my body . . ." (Luke 22:19). Now there have been different emphases put on that.

The Roman Catholic Church puts the emphasis upon *this. This* is My body. They say that transubstantiation takes place, that the bread becomes the flesh of Christ. Well, I don't think our Lord taught cannibalism in any form, shape, or fashion. I think, of course, that it is a wrong emphasis. Then there are those who have taken the position of the Lutheran church, which is consubstantiation. This means that *by, with, in, through,* and *under* the bread you get the body of Christ. Again, may I say, I think that falls short of what our Lord really means. Then there are those who take Zwingli's position. He was the Swiss Reformation leader who gave it a spiritual interpretation. He felt it was just a symbol, just a religious ritual, and that is all. I think that is probably the interpretation that most of Protestantism gives to it today. Frankly, I feel that falls as far short of the interpretation of the Lord's Supper as the other two do. Calvin put the emphasis on *is*—"This *is* my body." The Reformed faith has always put the emphasis there, and the early church put the emphasis there. The bread is bread, and it always will be bread. It cannot be changed. The wine is always just what it is, and there is no miracle that takes place there. You don't get the body of Christ by going through the ritual. And yet, it is more than a ritual. I had a seminary professor who taught us that in the Lord's Supper it is bread in your mouth, but it is Christ in your heart. Friend, I believe that there is a spiritual blessing that comes in observing the Lord's Supper. I think that He ministers to you spiritually through your obedience in observing the Lord's Supper. There is no such thing as a hocus–pocus there. Nor is it just an idle ritual that we go through. It is meaningful, and it has a spiritual blessing for the heart.

I think that is what our Lord is saying to them here. An intimate, real relationship with Him is the important thing. When they ate manna in the wilderness, it was only a temporary thing. Jesus has something that is eternal—*life* which is eternal. We are told that at the beginning of this Gospel, "In him was life; and the life was the light of men" (John 1:4).

These things said he in the synagogue, as he taught in Capernaum.

Many therefore of his disciples, when they had heard this, said, This is an hard saying; who can hear it?

When Jesus knew in himself that his disciples murmured at it, he said unto them, Doth this offend you?

What and if ye shall see the Son of man ascend up where he was before?

It is the spirit that quickeneth; the flesh profiteth nothing: the words that I speak unto you, they are spirit, and they are life [John 6:59-63].

There was definite reaction to what Jesus had said and differences of opinion. Jesus tells them that they are not going to eat Him literally because He is going back to heaven. It is the Spirit that makes alive; the flesh profits nothing. So obviously, friend, He is not talking about His literal body. We are to appropriate the Lord's Supper by faith. The juice in the cup is sweet, and I always taste the sweetness, remembering that He bore the bitter cup for me on the Cross so that I might have this sweet cup. That sweet cup is to remind me that He shed His blood for me, and there is a spiritual blessing there.

"The words that I speak unto you, they are spirit, and they are life." During my ministry, I have always read to the congregation from the Word of God during the Lord's Supper. I find that the Word of God ministers to the hearts of the people. Why? Because the words of the Lord Jesus are spirit and they are life.

But there are some of you that believe not. For Jesus knew from the beginning who they were that believed not, and who should betray him.

And he said, Therefore said I unto you, that no man can come unto me, except it were given unto him of my Father [John 6:64-65].

But remember now, you have to put with that "whosoever will may come." It's up to you, you see.

From that time many of his disciples went back, and walked no more with him [John 6:66].

You can see that in the group there that day were the hostile leaders, the religious leaders. Also there was an undesignated number of disciples in addition to the Twelve. And in the Twelve was Judas. So you actually find four opinions concerning Him at this time. Many of these disciples—not the Twelve—but many of the other disciples turned and went back.

Then said Jesus unto the twelve, will ye also go away?

Then Simon Peter answered him, Lord, to whom shall we go? thou hast the words of eternal life [John 6:67–68].

This is a marvelous statement on the part of Simon Peter. And the question he asks is pertinent to us today. If you say that the Lord Jesus is not a Savior to you and that He doesn't meet your needs at all, then may I ask you where you are going? I saw a group of young people on the island of Maui, out in the Hawaiian Islands. They had a picture of Krishna in front of them, and they were going over and over a monotonous song. Poor little folk! They weren't finding any satisfaction in that. What disillusionment is coming to so many today! There are those who are turning in every direction for light. Let me ask you the question of Simon Peter: "To whom shall we go?" The Lord Jesus is the One, and the only One, who has the Words of eternal life.

And we believe and are sure that thou art that Christ, the Son of the living God.

Jesus answered them, Have I not chosen you twelve, and one of you is a devil?

He spake of Judas Iscariot the son of Simon: for he it was that should betray him, being one of the twelve [John 6:69–71].

This man, Judas Iscariot, is really a great mystery. Here our Lord numbers him with the twelve and He said that He had chosen him. Yet he was a demon, which probably means demon–possessed, and this is the man who is going to betray Him. All the way through our Lord gave him every opportunity to make a decision for Him. It is difficult to interpret evil like this, friend. It is one of the mysteries.

Evil is always a mystery, which is one of the things that makes it so attractive. Suppose right now I would say to you that I am holding two sticks. One stick is perfectly straight because it is a ruler. You can easily imagine how that ruler looks because it can be straight only one way. Then suppose that I say that I am also holding in my hand a crooked stick. I'm of the opinion that if each of you drew a picture of how you think that stick looks, everyone would draw it differently. That's because it can be crooked in a million different ways. You see, evil has a mystery to it. I must confess that, as this man Judas Iscariot walks across the pages of Scripture, it's difficult to interpret him. And here our Lord says this amazing thing about him: he is a demon!

What a contrast is the testimony of Simon Peter—"we believe and are sure that thou art that Christ, the Son of the living God."

CHAPTER 7

THEME: *Jesus teaches at Feast of Tabernacles in temple (fifth word)*

This chapter contains the wonderful truths that Jesus is the Water of Life and that He promises to give the Holy Spirit to those who believe on Him.

JESUS TEACHES AT FEAST OF TABERNACLES IN TEMPLE (Fifth Word)

After these things Jesus walked in Galilee: for he would not walk in Jewry, because the Jews sought to kill him [John 7:1].

"After these things." This is a common expression with John who is giving us a chronological picture. The events of chapter 6 took place in Galilee at the Sea of Galilee; but before that, Jesus had been in Jerusalem where there had arisen the controversy concerning Him at the pool of Bethesda. It seems that the events of chapter 6 transpired about one year before the Cross in April; the events in chapter 7 occur about six months later, in October. Matthew 15—18 and Mark 7—9 and Luke 9 relate incidents which transpired during this period.

During the last year of His ministry, Jesus confined His activities to Galilee. It says that He walked no longer in Jewry, that means in Judaea, because the religious rulers there had a plot to kill Him. Jesus is following a divine schedule which His Father had given Him. These men could not touch Him until His time was come. We are now entering the last six months of His life, and the first incident which John records in that period is this occurrence of the Feast of Tabernacles.

Verse 1 reveals that a storm is gathering about the person of Christ. Six months later that storm will break in all its fury upon Jesus on the Cross. Friend, that storm is still going on. There is more difference of opinion about Him than about any other person who has ever lived. They blaspheme Him and say the worst things about Him that ever have been said. He's controversial today.

Although the storm is gathering, Jesus chose this time to abandon His method of staying away, and He went up to Jerusalem because it was the Feast of Tabernacles.

Now the Jews' feast of tabernacles was at hand [John 7:2].

There were three feasts which every male Jew was required to attend in Jerusalem. Our Lord kept the Law; He had to go up to Jerusalem during the Feasts of Passover, Tabernacles, and Pentecost. The Feast of Tabernacles is described in Leviticus 23. This was a feast of great joy to celebrate Israel's wonderful deliverance out of the land of Egypt. Because they had lived in tents during the wilderness journey, this is a feast of tents, or booths. They didn't have campers, you see, but they did camp out in booths. There was the blowing of trumpets and seventy bullocks were offered. There was the pouring out of water in the temple, with a double portion on the last day of the feast to remind them that God gave them water from the rock in the wilderness. They brought the water from the pool of Siloam and poured out literally barrels of water. During this festival, they illuminated the inner court with a regular torch parade. This was commemorating the pillar of fire that guided the children of Israel by night as they wandered in the wilderness. Now we can understand that the pillar of cloud and the pillar of fire that led the children of Israel were both pictures of our Lord Jesus Christ.

All the feasts of Jehovah in the Old Testament have been fulfilled except the Feast of Tabernacles. This will be fulfilled when our Lord returns to the earth. Thus it symbolizes the great joy of that time.

His brethren therefore said unto him, Depart hence, and go into Judaea, that thy disciples also may see the works that thou doest.

For there is no man that doeth any thing in secret, and he himself seeketh to be known openly. If thou do these things, shew thyself to the world.

For neither did his brethren believe in him [John 7:3–5].

These brethren are not His disciples but are His half–brothers. Their names are given to us in Matthew 13:55: James, Joses, Simon, and Judas. His half–brother, James, is the one who wrote the Epistle of James; His half–brother, Judas, probably is the one who wrote the Epistle of Jude. That was much later, of course, and at this point His brothers do not believe in Him. They are giving Him advice that He can't use at all.

Then Jesus said unto them, My time is not yet come: but your time is alway ready [John 7:6].

They are advising Jesus out of their unbelief, but Jesus does not take their advice. He is moving according to schedule, but it is His Father's schedule. He is not following the wisdom of the world, nor did He ever appeal to His own mind—it isn't that He doesn't think it is the right time to go. He is on a definite schedule from the Father; He is doing His Father's will.

Notice the little word *yet* in "My time is not *yet* come." Jesus did not say that He would not go down to the feast, but He was not going down with them publicly to win public favor by something spectacular, or whatever they wanted Him to do. He would go at His Father's appointed time and in His Father's way.

The world cannot hate you; but me it hateth, because I testify of it, that the works thereof are evil.

Go ye up unto this feast: I go not up yet unto this feast; for my time is not yet full come.

When he had said these words unto them, he abode still in Galilee [John 7:7–9].

The world is hostile to Christ. The reason is that our Lord Jesus Christ is the Light of the World. He turns on that Light, and that Light reveals everything that is wrong; it reveals sin. He condemns sin. That is the reason He is hated even today. He condemns sin by His very presence, by His very life. This raises a hostility in man because the heart of man is evil. Christ went to the Cross because He loved the human family. Redeeming love is what has broken the heart of hostile man.

We see this so clearly in the life of Saul of Tarsus. He was breathing out threatenings. He hated the Lord Jesus and anyone who followed Him. But when he came to know the Lord Jesus as his Savior, it broke his heart, and he could say, "He loved me, and gave himself for me" (see Gal. 3:20).

> **But when his brethren were gone up, then went he also up unto the feast, not openly, but as it were in secret [John 7:10].**

He probably traveled with His disciples on a back road and entered into the city through the sheep gate. I believe He always entered Jerusalem through the sheep gate until the time of His so–called triumphal entry when He appeared publicly, offering Himself to the nation and actually demanding that they either accept or reject Him.

> **Then the Jews sought him at the feast, and said, Where is he?**
>
> **And there was much murmuring among the people concerning him: for some said, He is a good man: others said, Nay; but he deceiveth the people.**
>
> **Howbeit no man spake openly of him for fear of the Jews [John 7:11–13].**

The "Jews" are the religious rulers—they were looking for Him and expecting Him because the Law required that He come to the feast. There was a lot of discussion concerning Him, but it was all done quite secretly because anyone would be attacked for making any statement that would be inclined in His favor and would be in danger of arrest.

Now about the midst of the feast Jesus went up into the temple, and taught [John 7:14].

Quite suddenly, He appeared in the temple. This Feast of Tabernacles is in the calendar of God and sets before us the coming of Christ in His return to earth and the events and stages which lead up to that. This feast speaks of the consummation of all things. He will appear suddenly. ". . . and the Lord, whom ye seek, shall suddenly come to his temple . . ." (Mal. 3:1). This will be fulfilled in His return to the earth.

And the Jews marvelled, saying, How knoweth this man letters, having never learned? [John 7:15].

Have you noticed how often we find Jesus teaching? Note the priority which He gave to the Word of God. The Jews (these would be the religious leaders) were astounded because He had no formal training in the rabbinical schools. They marveled that He could speak as He did. Even His enemies were forced to admit, "Never man spake like this man" (v. 46).

Jesus answered them, and said, My doctrine is not mine, but his that sent me [John 7:16].

To reject the message of Jesus is to reject the message of God. In chapters 4 and 5, He has insisted that to reject Him is to reject God. Don't ever tell me that He didn't make Himself equal with God. You may reject that He is, but you can never say that the Bible does not declare Him to be equal with God.

If any man will do his will, he shall know of the doctrine, whether it be of God, or whether I speak of myself [John 7:17].

"If anyone is willing to do His will" is the way Weymouth translates this. The Old Testament invites, "O taste and see that the LORD is good . . ." (Ps. 34:8). We have an adage that says, "The proof of the pudding is in the eating of it." Jesus invites you; come and make a laboratory test. "If any man will do his will, he shall know of the doctrine." There must be an attitude of love for the Word of God. Someone has said that human knowledge must be known to be loved, but divine knowledge must be loved to be understood. Here we have the steps: knowledge, love, obedience. That is what He asks you to do.

It's so easy to sit on the sidelines and be a Monday morning quarterback. We love to tell others how it should have been done or to speak our mind without really knowing. Jesus says, "Taste the Lord!" "If any man will do his will, he shall know of the doctrine, whether it be of God, or whether I speak of myself." That is the wonder of the Word of God. Friend, if you are willing, God will make it real to you. The Holy Spirit will confirm it to you.

He that speaketh of himself seeketh his own glory: but he that seeketh his glory that sent him, the same is true, and no unrighteousness is in him [John 7:18].

The question is whether men want to hear God. If they do, then God will speak to them in His Word. Then they will accept Jesus Christ who came to speak for the Father. Unfortunately, men are often more interested in a man who is seeking his own glory. If Jesus Christ had been trying to found some new cult, these men would have listened. But Jesus was not glorifying Himself; rather, He was giving all the glory to the Father and so ". . . the natural man receiveth not the things of the Spirit of God: for they are foolishness unto him: neither can he know them, because they are spiritually discerned" (1 Cor. 2:14). Therefore, some people read the Bible and get nothing out of it.

Did not Moses give you the law, and yet none of you keepeth the law? Why go ye about to kill me? [John 7:19].

Here is the hypocrisy of the legalist, the person who says the Sermon on the Mount is his religion or the person who says he lives by the Ten Commandments. The Lord Jesus says, "none of you keepeth the law." The Law is a mirror to let us see that we are lost sinners. The Law is important—don't misunderstand me—you don't kick the Law out the door. It expresses the will of God. But the purpose of the Law is to show us that we are sinners and that we need a Savior. The Law is a schoolmaster to bring us to Christ (see Gal. 3:24).

> **The people answered and said, Thou hast a devil: who goeth about to kill thee?**
>
> **Jesus answered and said unto them, I have done one work, and ye all marvel [John 7:20–21].**

Possibly they did not realize that there was a plot to put Jesus to death. Jesus refers to His work when He healed the man at the pool of Bethesda. This had aroused antagonism.

> **Moses therefore gave unto you circumcision; (not because it is of Moses, but of the fathers;) and ye on the sabbath day circumcise a man.**
>
> **If a man on the sabbath day receive circumcision, that the law of Moses should not be broken; are ye angry at me, because I have made a man every whit whole on the sabbath day?**
>
> **Judge not according to the appearance, but judge righteous judgment [John 7:22–24].**

Circumcision is a rite which goes back to Abraham and is older than the Mosaic Law. He is showing them their own inconsistency in their practice. In trying to keep the Law, they broke the Law. If a child was eight days old on the Sabbath Day, they would break the Sabbath Law and circumcise the child. They have no reply to this! Then Jesus warns them against making superficial judgments. That is still a difficulty with most of us today. We make superficial judgments because we don't have all the facts.

> Then said some of them of Jerusalem, Is not this he, whom they seek to kill?
>
> But, lo, he speaketh boldly, and they say nothing unto him. Do the rulers know indeed that this is the very Christ?
>
> Howbeit we know this man whence he is: but when Christ cometh, no man knoweth whence he is [John 7:25–27].

Again we note that there was a division concerning who Jesus is.

> Then cried Jesus in the temple as he taught, saying, Ye both know me, and ye know whence I am: and I am not come of myself, but he that sent me is true, whom ye know not.
>
> But I know him: for I am from him, and he hath sent me [John 7:28–29].

This is quite oratorical. Jesus is saying, "Do you really know Me? You think you know Me; you see Me, but you don't really know Me. You think you know where I have come from, but you don't really know."

> Then they sought to take him: but no man laid hands on him, because his hour was not yet come [John 7:30].

It's interesting that even though they were anxious to take Jesus, they couldn't touch Him until His hour had come.

> And many of the people believed on him, and said, When Christ cometh, will he do more miracles than these which this man hath done?

The Pharisees heard that the people murmured such things concerning him; and the Pharisees and the chief priests sent officers to take him.

Then said Jesus unto them, Yet a little while am I with you, and then I go unto him that sent me.

Ye shall seek me, and shall not find me: and where I am, thither ye cannot come [John 7:31–34].

Our Lord answered the Pharisees that they would take Him at the proper time—not until then. Then He tells them He will leave them. He is speaking of His resurrection and His ascension. They would never be able to touch Him again. Have you ever noticed that after His death upon the Cross, none but loving hands touched Him? None but loving eyes saw Him.

Then said the Jews among themselves, Whither will he go, that we shall not find him? will he go unto the dispersed among the Gentiles, and teach the Gentiles?

What manner of saying is this that he said, Ye shall seek me, and shall not find me: and where I am, thither ye cannot come? [John 7:35–36].

I think this is ridicule. They didn't think that Jesus could hide from them.

We come now to the last day of the feast, and it was on that day that they poured out a double portion of water in the temple. I think He could have been standing ankle deep in water when He said these words. They were celebrating the fact that God had given them water from the rock during the long trek of Israel through the wilderness. Paul tells us that the rock was Christ (see 1 Cor. 10:4). He is the One who gives the real water, the Water of Life.

In the last day, that great day of the feast, Jesus stood and cried, saying, If any man thirst, let him come unto me, and drink [John 7:37].

This is free will, friend. "If *any* man." That means you. God is offering a gift to you. Also here is election: "If any man thirst." The question is, "Are you thirsty?" Have you perhaps been drinking at the mud holes of the world, and have you been finding that they are not satisfying? "If any man thirst, let him come unto me, and drink." You can come to Him and receive Him as your Savior.

> **He that believeth on me, as the scripture hath said, out of his belly shall flow rivers of living water.**
>
> **(But this spake he of the Spirit, which they that believe on him should receive: for the Holy Ghost was not yet given; because that Jesus was not yet glorified.) [John 7:38–39].**

The Holy Spirit had not yet been given because Jesus was not yet glorified. The Holy Spirit did not come until the Day of Pentecost. Then He came to indwell believers and to form them into one body. The coming of the Holy Spirit on that day assures us that Jesus had arrived back at the Father's throne.

> **Many of the people therefore, when they heard this saying, said, Of a truth this is the Prophet [John 7:40].**

Some of the people believed and turned to Him. They drank and were satisfied.

> **Others said, This is the Christ. But some said, Shall Christ come out of Galilee? [John 7:41].**

We have the same thing today. Some believe, and some do not believe.

> **Hath not the scripture said, That Christ cometh of the seed of David, and out of the town of Bethlehem, where David was?**
>
> **So there was a division among the people because of him [John 7:42–43].**

He *was* of the seed of David and out of the town of Bethlehem. That was where He first touched down on this earth. It was "splashdown" for Him in that miserable little stable in that miserable little town. It's not like the pretty pictures you see on Christmas cards. He began in Bethlehem, but He didn't stay there for His earthly ministry. If these people had really wanted to know, they could have learned that His birth took place in Bethlehem and that He did fulfill the prophecies. He is the One who is giving them the invitation to come and drink, but they put up this objection. There will always be a division among the people over who He is until He comes to reign.

And some of them would have taken him; but no man laid hands on him [John 7:44].

They couldn't. His hour was not yet come.

Then came the officers to the chief priests and Pharisees; and they said unto them, Why have ye not brought him?

The officers answered, Never man spake like this man [John 7:45–46].

What a testimony these men gave about Jesus, "Never man spake like this man." He was *the* great teacher, but it is not by His teaching that we are saved. He saves us by His death and resurrection.

Then answered them the Pharisees, Are ye also deceived?

Have any of the rulers or of the Pharisees believed on him?

But this people who knoweth not the law are cursed.

Nicodemus saith unto them, (he that came to Jesus by night, being one of them,)

Doth our law judge any man, before it hear him, and know what he doeth?

They answered and said unto him, Art thou also of Galilee? Search, and look: for out of Galilee ariseth no prophet.

And every man went unto his own house [John 7:47–53].

This is the Nicodemus who came to Jesus by night. I think that Nicodemus trusted the Lord that night. He is a Pharisee, and he defends Jesus. They ridicule him with a joke, "Art thou also of Galilee?" That was a disgrace to them. It was like city folk making fun of the country folk. It is interesting to note that they did know the facts of their Scripture: "Out of Galilee ariseth no prophet." In the true sense He hadn't come out of Galilee, nor had He come out of Bethlehem. He had come out of glory. "Unto us a child is born, unto us a son is given" (Isa. 9:6)—the Son came out from heaven.

"Every man went unto his own house." No one invited Jesus into his home. It was a feast night, but Jesus went out to the Mount of Olives. As far as we know, He never spent a night in Jerusalem.

How about you, my friend? Do you go to your own home and leave Jesus out in the cold? Or have you accepted His wonderful invitation so that you live in the love and light of His presence?

CHAPTER 8

THEME: *Jesus in temple forgives woman taken in adultery (sixth word)*

The chapter opens with the episode of the woman taken in adultery. John uses his customary method of following an incident with a discourse. There was a sharp conflict between our Lord and the religious rulers relative to this woman and what should be done with her. Arising from this came the marvelous discourse on Jesus the Light of the World.

The episode of the woman, covering the first eleven verses, is not found in some of the better manuscripts. As I am sure you know, our English Bibles are translated from the original languages. The New Testament was first written in the Greek language. Extant manuscripts were used to compile a Greek New Testament; then our English translations were made from that. The Greek text of Westcott and Hort omits the incident of the woman taken in adultery from its position in the eighth chapter of John but inserts it at the end of that Gospel. Nestle's Greek text includes it but encloses it in brackets. Augustine writes that it was omitted because of a prudish fear that it would encourage adultery. However, if we read the account carefully, we will see that it does not condone sin. Rather, it condemns sin. We have both a scholarly and moral basis for considering it part of the inspired Word of God.

JESUS IN TEMPLE FORGIVES WOMAN TAKEN IN ADULTERY (Sixth Word)

Jesus went unto the mount of Olives.

And early in the morning he came again into the temple, and all the people came unto him; and he sat down, and taught them [John 8:1–2].

Remember that the night before there had been a meeting of the San-
hedrin and that people were divided in their opinion as to whether or
not Jesus was the Messiah. Nicodemus defended Him. Everyone had
gone home, and not one had invited Jesus to his house. Early in the
morning, He came back into Jerusalem, went back to the temple, and
sat down to teach.

> **And the scribes and Pharisees brought unto him a
> woman taken in adultery; and when they had set her in
> the midst,**
>
> **They say unto him, Master, this woman was taken in
> adultery, in the very act [John 8:3-4].**

What could be more crude and rude and brutal than this act of these
religious rulers? As our Lord was sitting in the temple area teaching
the people, there is a hullabaloo outside. Then here come these religious rulers dragging a woman with her clothes in disarray, her hair
all disheveled, defiant, and resisting them. The crowd would naturally turn and look to see what in the world was happening. The religious rulers bring her right into the midst of the group that the Lord
Jesus is teaching! They fling her down on the ground there and make
their crude charge. "This woman was taken in adultery, in the very
act."

She is guilty, there is no doubt about that. And what she did was
sin. Our Lord called it sin—He finally said to her, "Go, and sin no
more." They knew the Law perfectly well: "And the man that committeth adultery with another man's wife, even he that committeth adultery with his neighbour's wife, the adulterer and the adulteress shall
surely be put to death" (Lev. 20:10). Where was the man? The very
fact that they did not produce the man also makes it apparent that they
were not interested in enforcing the Law. They had another motive.

> **Now Moses in the law commanded us, that such should
> be stoned: but what sayest thou?**

This they said, tempting him, that they might have to accuse him. But Jesus stooped down, and with his finger wrote on the ground, as though he heard them not [John 8:5-6].

They are right about the Law of Moses; there is no way of toning it down. She should be stoned. They are putting Him on the horns of a dilemma. Will He contradict Moses? Will he say something else, offer some other explanation? They did this to trap Him so that they might accuse Him. They didn't really want to stone the woman. They wanted to stone *Him*. Our Lord knew that, of course—He "needed not that any should testify of man: for he knew what was in man" (John 2:25).

This scene is very interesting. The defiant woman is flung before Him. The crowd has no respect for her embarrassment, her feelings, and they leer at her and crane their necks to see her, adding to her humiliation.

Jesus stoops and writes on the ground. In effect, He dismisses the case. He will not join with her accusers. He will not so much as look at her to add to her embarrassment. He stoops down and writes as though He doesn't even hear them.

This is the only record that we have of His writing anything. He is the One about whom more books have been written, pro and con, than about any other person who has ever lived; yet He never wrote anything except this in the sands of the temple floor, which the wind or the feet of the crowd erased.

What did He write? Of course we don't know, but I can make a suggestion. Turning back to the prophets, we pick up something quite interesting: "O LORD, the hope of Israel, all that forsake thee shall be ashamed, and they that depart from me shall be written in the earth, because they have forsaken the LORD, the fountain of living waters" (Jer. 17:13). Now, who had forsaken the Lord? This woman? Yes, she had. The religious rulers? Yes, they had. Their names shall be written in the earth. This is what I think He wrote, linking their names with sins of their past. Perhaps He wrote the name of a woman living in Rome. One old pious Pharisee had had an affair in Rome when he was a young fellow. His wife didn't know about it; no one in Jerusalem knew about it; but our Lord knew that old rascal. As He just wrote the name of the woman, the old Pharisee came over and saw it—and suddenly remembered that he had another appointment. Perhaps one of the scribes made regular trips to Ephesus, a great sinning place, to a certain address over there which Jesus wrote in the sand. The scribe looked at it and said, "Oh, my gracious!" He left hurriedly. Another scribe may have left a girl in Galilee who was pregnant. He didn't marry her, and he didn't think anyone knew. Our Lord wrote the name of the girl and the scribe's name with it.

"Thou hast set our iniquities before thee, our secret sins in the light of thy countenance" (Ps. 90:8). Secret sin on earth is open scandal in heaven.

> **So when they continued asking him, he lifted up himself, and said unto them, He that is without sin among you, let him first cast a stone at her.**
>
> **And again he stooped down, and wrote on the ground.**
>
> **And they which heard it, being convicted by their own conscience, went out one by one, beginning at the eldest, even unto the last: and Jesus was left alone, and the woman standing in the midst [John 8:7–9].**

Jesus gives the requirements for being a judge, which is something for all of us to hear. We have the right to be the judge of others provided we meet the requirement. That requirement is *sinlessness*. May I say to you, my friend, I don't know about you, but that takes me out of the stone–throwing business.

An old Scottish commentator says that the elder ones left first because they had more sense than the younger ones. The younger ones hung around until they saw their own names come up, and then they finally caught on and left also. So there was not a person left there who could throw a stone at her except One. Only Jesus could have thrown the stone at her. All the others had slinked away. What hypocrites they were!

When Jesus had lifted up himself, and saw none but the woman, he said unto her, Woman, where are those thine accusers? hath no man condemned thee?

She said, No man, Lord. And Jesus said unto her, Neither do I condemn thee: go, and sin no more [John 8:10–11].

This woman was guilty of sin, and according to the Law of Moses an adulteress was to be put to death. Is Jesus reversing the Mosaic system? No. He is placing His Cross between that woman and her sin. This One who is the Son of the virgin, who Himself was under a cloud all of His life, is going to the Cross to pay the penalty for even the sin of this woman. He did not come into the world to condemn the world. He did not come to judge this woman. He came into the world to be a Savior!

A great many people think they are lost because they have committed a certain sin. I have news for you. One is not lost because he is a murderer, or a liar, or a thief, or an adulterer, or because he has borne false witness or committed other sins. A person does these things because he is lost and does not believe in Jesus Christ. Jesus Christ forgives sins. He is the Savior. He died for the sins of the whole world. Any person who comes to the Lord Jesus Christ is forgiven.

JESUS IS THE LIGHT OF THE WORLD (Sixth Word)

We notice that Jesus often follows this method. After an incident or a miracle, He gives a discourse on that subject.

Then spake Jesus again unto them, saying, I am the light of the world: he that followeth me shall not walk in darkness, but shall have the light of life [John 8:12].

Notice He says, "I am"—this "I am" occurs again and again. In the Old Testament, Jehovah is the ". . . I AM THAT I AM . . ." (Exod. 3:14). Very frankly, we are told very little about God. We know He is the self–

existing One, that He has all wisdom and all power. The Lord Jesus came to this earth not only to redeem man but also to reveal God to man. Jesus greatly expands our understanding by using the commonplace things like bread, light, and water to symbolize Himself. He uses the ordinary to speak of the extraordinary, the physical to speak of the spiritual, the temporal to speak of the eternal, the here-and-now to speak of the hereafter, the earthly to speak of the heavenly, the limited to speak of the unlimited, and the finite to speak of the infinite. Jesus gives us a revelation of God when He tells us that He is Bread, He is Water, He is Life. Then we understand that not only is God self-existing, but that He also meets our every need. Jesus said, "I am the bread of life" (John 6:35), "I am the light of the world" (John 8:12), "I am the door" (John 10:9), "I am the good shepherd" (John 10:11), "I am the resurrection, and the life" (John 11:25), "I am the way, the truth, and the life" (John 14:6), and "I am the vine, ye are the branches" (John 15:5).

Here Jesus is saying, "I am the light of the world." He has just exposed the sin of the scribes and the Pharisees who brought the woman guilty of adultery. Because they were just as guilty as she, they had to flee. When one turns on the light, all the rats, the bats, and the bedbugs crawl away. Light exposes sin, which is the reason the scribes and the Pharisees had to leave.

"I am the light of the world" is the highest claim that He has made so far in the Gospel of John. One of the definitions of God is that He is Light (see 1 John 1:5). He is absolute in His holiness and in His justice. Even physical light is one of the most complicated things as well as one of the most essential things for us. Who really knows what it is? In some ways it acts like waves, and in some ways it acts like particles of matter. The startling thing is that men, acting on both of these definitions or principles, have been able to make remarkable inventions and discoveries. Some say that both are true and yet others say both can't be true. Is light the absence of darkness? Is darkness the absence of light? We say a room is filled with light. What do we mean? Does it weigh any more when it is filled with light? There could be no such thing as color without light. The red rose is red because it has absorbed every other part of light except red. That is the reason we see red in the red rose.

We don't understand light, and certainly a child doesn't understand light, but he does know enough about it to turn on the light switch when he enters a dark room. Jesus Christ is the Light of the World. Just as the sun is the physical light of this world, He is spiritual Light. Just as a little child can have enough sense to come into the presence of light, so any sinner today, though he be "a fool and a wayfaring man" (see Isa. 35:8), can come into the presence of the Lord Jesus Christ.

There are those who deny that Christ is the Light of the World. They are walking in a lesser light. As the moon has no light of its own but reflects light from the sun, so this civilization that we live in today owes everything to Christ. We have hospitals, charities, orphans' homes, consideration for the poor, rights of labor because the Lord Jesus came to this earth. The reason we have problems in these areas today is that we have wandered too far from the Light. The world is just walking in moonlight, as it were. How this poor old world needs to get back to the Light which is Christ.

"He that followeth me shall not walk in darkness, but shall have the light of life." There are those who have attempted to liken Jesus the Light to the headlights of a car. Friend, the headlights of a car do not lead anywhere. Who does the leading?—The fellow at the steering wheel. Unfortunately, this is the way many Christians try to live their lives. I don't consider this an apt illustration of Christ.

During this Feast of Tabernacles, Israel was remembering the deliverance when the pillar of fire led the children of Israel through the wilderness. They were celebrating this with a torch parade. When Jesus said, "I am the light of the world," this is what He was referring to. Whenever and wherever the pillar of fire led, the children of Israel followed. We are to follow Him in like manner, looking to Him as the Light of the World.

The Pharisees therefore said unto him, Thou bearest record of thyself; thy record is not true.

> Jesus answered and said unto them, Though I bear
> record of myself, yet my record is true: for I know
> whence I came, and whither I go; but ye cannot tell
> whence I come, and whither I go [John 8:13-14].

There is now a sharp conflict between the religious rulers and Christ.
They are really accusing Him of boasting when He claimed to be the
Light. Jesus gives them a threefold reason why His testimony is true.

First, He says, "I know whence I came." He says He knows where
He came from and, hence, He knows Himself. By the way, folk on this
earth can't tell you where they came from. Scientists try to tell us
what has happened millions of years ago; yet none of them were here
even one hundred years ago. They don't *know* where they came from;
they can only speculate. But the Lord Jesus knew from where He
came.

> Ye judge after the flesh; I judge no man.
>
> And yet if I judge, my judgment is true: for I am not
> alone, but I and the Father that sent me [John 8:15-16].

His second statement is that He judges no man after the flesh. Any
judgment that you or I make is after the flesh. Our judgment is limited
because we simply do not have all the facts. The theory of evolution is
an example of this. Because our judgments are based on very fragmen-
tary facts, they really are speculation. Either man accepts speculation
or he accepts revelation. If one judges according to the flesh, he will
naturally follow speculation. The Lord Jesus says that *He* does not
judge according to the flesh. He gives the judgment that comes from
heaven. He gives God's viewpoint, God's estimation. This is revelation, and it differs from man's point of view. That is why the hostility
of these religious rulers is mounting.

> It is also written in your law, that the testimony of two
> men is true.
>
> I am one that bear witness of myself, and the Father that
> sent me beareth witness of me [John 8:17-18].

Here is the third reason that His testimony is true. The Father had borne witness to Him. They had heard the Father's voice out of heaven.

> **Then said they unto him, Where is thy Father? Jesus answered, Ye neither know me, nor my Father: if ye had known me, ye should have known my Father also [John 8:19].**

They are reflecting on His birth again. Notice that Jesus calls God "my Father" in a different relationship from what you and I have with Him through faith in Christ. Remember, He said to Mary after His resurrection, "I ascend unto my Father, and your Father" (John 20:17). We become children of God through faith in Jesus Christ, but Jesus is His Son because of His position in the Trinity. He is God the Son, and He addresses God the Father. This has nothing to do with generation or regeneration, but it has everything to do with His position in the Trinity.

"If ye had known me, ye should have known my Father also." Here is the cleavage. Here is the real issue. There is no middle ground. If you are going to know God the Father, you must come through Jesus Christ. There is no other way.

> **These words spake Jesus in the treasury, as he taught in the temple: and no man laid hands on him; for his hour was not yet come.**
>
> **Then said Jesus again unto them, I go my way, and ye shall seek me, and shall die in your sins: whither I go, ye cannot come.**
>
> **Then said the Jews, Will he kill himself? because he saith, Whither I go, ye cannot come [John 8:20–22].**

The treasury was in the women's court. This was where they had brought the woman taken in adultery. You will notice how much these Jews were in the dark. First they ask, "Where is thy Father?" Now they ask, "Will he kill himself?" They know nothing about the fact that He has been instructing His own that He is going to Jerusalem to die at the hands of the Gentiles, that He will be delivered up to die by these very same religious rulers, and that He will die a redemptive death for the sins of the world. Will He kill Himself? No! He will give Himself a ransom for many.

> **And he said unto them, Ye are from beneath; I am from above: ye are of this world; I am not of this world [John 8:23].**

We find this same thought in 1 Corinthians 2:14. Human knowledge can be understood by any other man who has a human nature—if his IQ is high enough. But divine knowledge is different. Only the Spirit of God can take the things of Christ and show them to us. That's what He is saying here.

> **I said therefore unto you, that ye shall die in your sins: for if ye believe not that I am he, ye shall die in your sins [John 8:24].**

People die because they are sinners. That is the natural consequence of sin. "If ye believe not that I am he, ye shall die in your sins." Can a person be saved on his deathbed? Yes, if he accepts the Lord Jesus Christ as his Savior. But a person can reject Christ too long, just as these Jews did. There comes a time when one has rejected Christ too long and then will not ever want to accept Him.

> **Then said they unto him, Who art thou? And Jesus saith unto them, Even the same that I said unto you from the beginning [John 8:25].**

These Jews did not know what His mission was, His work was, nor did they know Him. "Where is thy Father?" "Will He kill Himself?" "Who art Thou?" Jesus answers that His statement concerning Himself is always the same. He consistently claims that He is the Messiah, the Savior of the world.

> **I have many things to say and to judge of you: but he that sent me is true; and I speak to the world those things which I have heard of him [John 8:26].**

Our Lord always maintained that what He was doing and saying was what the Father wanted Him to do and say. He claimed that God the Father had sent Him and that He was doing the Father's will. He never appealed to His own mind or His own intellect. This is an example for us who are preachers. It is God's Word that we are to be giving out rather than messages that are the product of our own intellects.

> **They understood not that he spake to them of the Father [John 8:27].**

They missed the whole point. They are of the earth; they do not understand heavenly things.

> **Then said Jesus unto them, When ye have lifted up the Son of man, then shall ye know that I am he, and that I do nothing of myself; but as my Father hath taught me, I speak these things [John 8:28].**

When Jesus calls Himself the Son of Man, He is referring to Daniel 7:13–14. The Son of Man comes to the Ancient of Days to be made ruler of this universe. So the Lord Jesus is referring here to His crucifixion and also to His crowning that is yet to come.

After the death and resurrection of Christ, many of these religious rulers believed. We are told in the Book of Acts that many of the priests in Jerusalem believed. This is what He is saying to them now. Afterwards they would know that He is the One He claims to be. It is the redemptive death of Christ that explains Him, why He came and who He is. One cannot really know who He is until one knows what He has done.

> And he that sent me is with me: the Father hath not left
> me alone; for I do always those things that please him.
>
> As he spake these words, many believed on him [John
> 8:29–30].

Have you ever finished a day without looking back on it and wishing that you had done some things a little differently? Our Lord never finished a day with a regret. He always did those things that pleased His Father. He is making it abundantly clear that He has come to do the Father's will.

> Then said Jesus to those Jews which believed on him, If
> ye continue in my word, then are ye my disciples in-
> deed;
>
> And ye shall know the truth, and the truth shall make
> you free [John 8:31–32].

Faith alone saves, but the faith that saves is not alone. It will produce something. After a person believes on the Lord Jesus Christ, he will want to "continue in His Word." The proof of faith is continuing with the Savior. As the pastor of a church, I learned to watch out for the person who is active in the church but is not interested in the study of the Word of God. Such a one is dangerous to a church.

The truth shall make you free. The truth is that Jesus Christ is the Savior of the world. He is the Truth. First we come to Him as our Savior. Then as we go on with Him, we know by experience that we are free. We are free from the penalty of sin—we don't need to lie awake at night worrying about going to hell. He doesn't even ask us to live the Christian life. He asks us to trust Him and let Him live His life through us. When we yield to Him, we are free.

> They answered him, We be Abraham's seed, and were
> never in bondage to any man: how sayest thou, Ye shall
> be made free? [John 8:33].

They lied when they said that. They had been in bondage in Egypt and in Babylon, and as they spoke, they were under the iron heel of Rome. What a misrepresentation that was.

> **Jesus answered them, Verily, verily, I say unto you, Whosoever committeth sin is the servant of sin.**
>
> **And the servant abideth not in the house for ever: but the Son abideth ever.**
>
> **If the Son therefore shall make you free, ye shall be free indeed.**
>
> **I know that ye are Abraham's seed; but ye seek to kill me, because my word hath no place in you.**
>
> **I speak that which I have seen with my Father: and ye do that which ye have seen with your father [John 8:34–38].**

They were not free physically, and they were not free spiritually. They claimed to be Abraham's seed; yet they sought to kill Jesus.

"Whosoever committeth sin is the servant of sin" is in the present tense. If you continue in a life of sin, you are a servant of sin. I doubt if any of us go through one day without sinning, but the child of God comes to the Father every day and confesses his sin. The child of the Devil will never do that. This is the thought of Romans 6:16, "Know ye not, that to whom ye yield yourselves servants to obey, his servants ye are to whom ye obey . . . ?"

Jesus gets rather subtle now. A servant may come and work for you during the day, but when evening comes, he gets his hat and goes home. The son comes in, pitches his hat in a corner, sits down and relaxes because he is the son. The Lord was telling these rulers that they are not really God's children. They were in the temple then, but they wouldn't be there long. In A.D. 70 Titus came and took every one of them away and sold them into slavery. The five o'clock whistle had blown, and the servants left the house.

The Son makes us free indeed. We do not have to be the servant of sin. Many Christians accept defeat and failure as a normal Christian life. God never intended us to live like that. He intends us to live for Him by the power of the Holy Spirit.

> **They answered and said unto him, Abraham is our father. Jesus saith unto them, If ye were Abraham's children, ye would do the works of Abraham.**
>
> **But now ye seek to kill me, a man that hath told you the truth, which I have heard of God: this did not Abraham.**
>
> **Ye do the deeds of your father. Then said they to him, We be not born of fornication; we have one Father, even God.**
>
> **Jesus said unto them, If God were your Father, ye would love me: for I proceeded forth and came from God; neither came I of myself, but he sent me.**
>
> **Why do ye not understand my speech? even because ye cannot hear my word.**
>
> **Ye are of your father the devil, and the lusts of your father ye will do. He was a murderer from the beginning, and abode not in the truth, because there is no truth in him. When he speaketh a lie, he speaketh of his own: for he is a liar, and the father of it [John 8:39–44].**

The old adage says, "Like father, like son." Although they claim that they are the children of Abraham, Jesus tells these men that if they were truly the children of Abraham, they would act like Abraham. Instead, they are trying to kill Him. So instead of being the children of Abraham, they are, in fact, the children of the Devil. Satan is the originator of murder and of lying, and they were being his imitators, his children. "Ye do the deeds of your father."

Notice that they again bring up the subject, "We be not born of fornication." When I first entered the ministry, I took the position that one could deny the virgin birth and still be a Christian. I don't do so today. If we deny the virgin birth of Christ, I believe we are joining this taunting crowd who said, "We be not born of fornication." Yet, this crowd want to claim that God is their Father. Jesus says, "If God were your Father, ye would love me: for I proceeded forth and came from God; neither came I of myself, but he sent me."

How do *we* know that God is our Father? John, in his epistle, gives us this answer: "Whosoever believeth that Jesus is the Christ is born of God: and every one that loveth him that begat loveth him also that is begotten of him" (1 John 5:1).

These Jews thought they were the children of God when they were actually the children of the Devil. We find the same idea today. This doctrine of the universal fatherhood of God and the universal brotherhood of man has brought us into a lot of trouble. It has shaped the philosophy of our nation. We sit down at a conference table with the children of the Devil, and we call them the children of God. I am afraid that our nation has been deceived by other nations of the world because our wise diplomats and smart politicians are simply working on the wrong premise. The Bible does not teach the universal fatherhood of God and the universal brotherhood of man. Obviously Jesus did not teach the universal fatherhood of God because He was saying to these religious rulers that they were children of the *Devil.* Apparently, there are some people who are not the children of God! One becomes a child of God only through faith in the Lord Jesus Christ.

The words of Jesus antagonized these men. Yet, Jesus insisted that His words are truth. He also insisted that none of them could convince Him of sin. Jesus is from God, and anyone who is a child of God will listen to Jesus Christ. People still don't like to hear that today. Folk try to think we're all nice, sweet brothers to each other, and they talk of love, love, love. My friend, if you are going to stand for the *truth* today, then you will denounce the evil just as our Lord did. That is going to bring antagonism.

And because I tell you the truth, ye believe me not [John 8:45].

Isn't it interesting that Jesus can tell people the truth and they will not believe. It arouses their intense antagonism. Yet people will believe the wildest rumors and the biggest lies. Dictators have learned that. Hitler was very frank about this in his book when he said that if a big lie is told again and again and again, finally the people will believe it. Today advertisers and the news media have learned this also.

> **Which of you convinceth me of sin? And if I say the truth, why do ye not believe me?**
>
> **He that is of God heareth God's words: ye therefore hear them not, because ye are not of God.**
>
> **Then answered the Jews, and said unto him, Say we not well that thou art a Samaritan, and hast a devil? [John 8:46–48].**

Jesus put His very life on the line when He asked, "Which of you convinceth me of sin?" This is one of the great proofs of the deity of Christ. Believe me, if any of His enemies had had one shred of evidence against Him, they would have used it. They have no logical answers for His questions. So what do they do? They come up with ridicule. I learned this method long ago when I was on a debate team. When they have no logical answer, they resort to ridicule. Listen to the Jews. "You're a Samaritan; you have a demon"—as I'm sure you know, demon is the correct translation. This is name-calling and pure ridicule.

> **Jesus answered, I have not a devil; but I honour my Father, and ye do dishonour me.**
>
> **And I seek not mine own glory: there is one that seeketh and judgeth.**
>
> **Verily, verily, I say unto you, If a man keep my saying, he shall never see death [John 8:49–51].**

I wish we could see Him standing in that crowd. They hate Him so much that they want to kill Him. They have murder in their hearts, and He has nothing but love in His. He is going to go to the Cross to die for them. They are thinking of death for Him, but He is offering them life. "If a man keep my saying, he shall never see death." He is offering them eternal life, spiritual life. My friend, this Jesus is more than a man.

> **Then said the Jews unto him, Now we know that thou hast a devil. Abraham is dead, and the prophets; and thou sayest, If a man keep my saying, he shall never taste of death.**

> **Art thou greater than our father Abraham, which is dead? and the prophets are dead: whom makest thou thyself?**

> **Jesus answered, If I honour myself, my honour is nothing: it is my Father that honoureth me; of whom ye say, that he is your God:**

> **Yet ye have not known him; but I know him: and if I should say, I know him not, I shall be a liar like unto you: but I know him, and keep his saying.**

> **Your father Abraham rejoiced to see my day: and he saw it, and was glad.**

> **Then said the Jews unto him, Thou art not yet fifty years old, and hast thou seen Abraham?**

> **Jesus said unto them, Verily, verily I say unto you, Before Abraham was, I am.**

> **Then took they up stones to cast at him: but Jesus hid himself, and went out of the temple, going through the midst of them, and so passed by [John 8:52–59].**

Did Abraham ever see Christ? He certainly did. The appearance of God to people in the Old Testament was an appearance of Jesus Christ to these people. "No man hath seen God at any time; the only begotten

Son, which is in the bosom of the Father, he hath declared him" (John 1:18). Then, too, although Abraham's body was buried there, yet Abraham was really not dead but was in the presence of God. Jesus makes this very clear, as recorded in Luke 20:38. "For he is not a God of the dead, but of the living: for all live unto him."

The liberal theologian today teaches that Jesus Christ was a great teacher but that He never really claimed to be God. My friend, listen to this. "Before Abraham was, I am." Not, I *was*—I *AM*. He is the Jehovah, the I AM, God. The Jews understood perfectly. Because they knew precisely what He was claiming, they took up stones to kill Him for blasphemy.

The issue is Jesus Christ. He put these Jews on the spot. They had to make a decision concerning Him. You must make a decision concerning Him. Either He is the Truth or He is a liar. Either He is God and Savior, or He is not. You must decide. Either you accept Him or you reject Him. Remember that your decision does not in any way change who He is. He is the great I AM, Jehovah, the eternal God. Your decision is to accept or deny this.

CHAPTER 9

THEME: Jesus opens the eyes of a man born blind in Jerusalem (fifth work); record of the miracle; reaction to the miracle

The Lord has been giving His discourse on the Light of the World. Because He claimed that He is God, the Jews wanted to kill Him. Jesus "hid" Himself as He went out of the temple, "going through the midst of them" (John 8:59). It was a miracle that He could escape this angry mob. His time had not yet come, and so they could not lay their hands on Him.

The incident which now follows is still really a continuation of the discourse on the Light of the World. The enemies of the Lord Jesus could not see because they were spiritually blind. The blind man also could not see, even when the Light of the World stood before him, but Jesus is going to reveal Himself to him. Before the blind man can see, he must have his eyes restored. Light must be received. There must be a receiver as well as a sender of Light.

We used to argue the question about noise. If a tree falls in the forest and nobody is there to hear it, is there a noise? The obvious answer is that there are sound waves, but if there is no ear there to pick up the sound and interpret it, no one hears it as noise. There must be a receiver.

The lack of sight does not mean that light is not there. Light reveals the condition of the eye. The Light of the World reveals the condition of the soul. The Pharisees thought they saw, but they were blind.

There is a story of a mining explosion in West Virginia. The explosion plunged the trapped men into total darkness. When the rescue team managed to get a light through to them, one of the young men finally said, "Well, why don't they turn on the light?" They all looked at him in amazement, and then they realized that the explosion had blinded him. In the darkness, he did not know that he was blind. The light revealed to him and to them that he was blind.

This is what Jesus means in verse 39 of this chapter: "For judgment I am come into this world, that they which see not might see; and that they which see might be made blind." Light reveals the true condition. Those who are blind, but do not realize it, can know that they are truly blind.

A prominent member of the English Parliament took Mr. Burke, who was a statesman and a great orator, to hear Dr. Black, one of the great preachers of Scotland. Dr. Black preached a powerful sermon exalting the Lord Jesus Christ. After the service the friend waited for Mr. Burke's reaction to the message. Finally he said, "He is a great orator, but what was he talking about?" Here was a brilliant man who was blind.

It is our responsibility to get out the Word of God, and there our responsibility ends. It is the work of the Holy Spirit to open the heart of the listener and cause him to obey the Word. We should present the Light of the World to people, but the Holy Spirit must open the eyes. This is what is meant in 2 Corinthians 2:15–16: "For we are unto God a sweet savour of Christ, in them that are saved, and in them that perish: To the one we are the savour of death unto death; and to the other the savour of life unto life . . ." We are equally as "successful" when we do not win a convert as when we do. We are simply to shine the light, to hold up Jesus Christ, the Light of the World. One fellow will say to us, "Where is the light? That doesn't make sense to me." We will look at him and say, "Poor fellow, he is blind." Another fellow will say to us, "Thank you for showing me the light. I was blind but now I see."

JESUS OPENS THE EYES OF A MAN BORN BLIND IN JERUSALEM (Fifth Work)

And as Jesus passed by, he saw a man which was blind from his birth [John 9:1].

Logically this episode of the blind man follows the wonderful statement of our Lord, "I am the light of the world" (John 8:12). There evidently was a lapse of time between chapter 8 and the opening of chapter 9 because He is moving in a more leisurely manner—"as Jesus passed by."

RECORD OF THE MIRACLE

This is the only record of our Lord healing a man with congenital blindness.

And his disciples asked him, saying, Master, who did sin, this man, or his parents, that he was born blind? [John 9:2].

The disciples want to establish the cause of his disease. They want to discuss who is at fault, who it is that sinned. In their day there were probably four answers they would have given. The pagans of that day, as many of today also, believed in reincarnation and held that congenital disease could be the result of sins committed during a former existence. The Jews never did accept this explanation. Then there is the argument of heredity, that the sins of the fathers are visited upon the children to the third and fourth generations (see Exod. 20:5). We know that this is possible and that blindness in some cases can be the result of the sin of the parent. Then, there was the explanation that the sin of Adam was passed to each member of the human family so that all are subject to death and disease. And finally, the Jewish rabbis believed that a child in the womb could sin.

Jesus answered, Neither hath this man sinned, nor his parents: but that the works of God should be made manifest in him.

I must work the works of him that sent me, while it is day: the night cometh, when no man can work.

As long as I am in the world, I am the light of the world [John 9:3–5].

Jesus doesn't give them the answer they wanted. He says the important thing is not to probe around in the past and try to find out who is guilty. The thing to do is to cure the man. It may be true that an ounce of prevention is worth a pound of cure, but after a man is sick, it's pretty important to get that pound of cure for him.

God has His own wise reasons for permitting sickness, disease, suffering, and trouble. When I went to the hospital for surgery, I received letters from hundreds of people. Out of those letters, there were several who proposed to tell me why God let this happen to me. The only trouble was, I don't think that any one of them knew. God doesn't always reveal to us why He permits things. I believe this:

> God never does, nor suffers to be done
> But what we would ourselves,
> Could we but see through all events of things
> As well as He.

God has His way, and He doesn't propose to tell us all His reasons. He does ask us to walk with Him by faith through the dark times of our lives.

I think, frankly, that we need to understand that our Lord is not saying for one minute that this man was sort of a spiritual guinea pig. I believe the punctuation of the verse misleads us. Jesus is saying, "Neither hath this man sinned, nor his parents. But that the works of God should be made manifest in him, I must work the works of Him that sent me, while it is day."

God has created you and me for His glory. He did not create us that we might try to be a somebody down here. He created us for *His* glory. If we miss that, we miss the entire purpose of our creation. These trials and sufferings come to us because they bring about the glory of God. This blind man, through the healing of his blindness, will bring about the glory of God. Not only will this blind man see (and think how much he would *enjoy* seeing all the rest of his life), but also he will see Jesus Christ and come to know Him as his Savior.

Now Jesus reverts to His original statement. "I am the light of the world." The night makes all of mankind blind. No one can see. Christ is the spiritual Light of the World, and without Him everyone is blind. But as long as He is in the world, He is the Light of the World. He is still in the world today, my friend. He comes to us in the person of the Holy Spirit. Unless the Son of God, by means of the Holy Spirit, opens our eyes so that we can see spiritual things, we will remain blind as bats.

When he had thus spoken, he spat on the ground, and made clay of the spittle, and he anointed the eyes of the blind man with the clay,

And said unto him, Go, wash in the pool of Siloam, (which is by interpretation, Sent.) He went his way therefore, and washed, and came seeing [John 9:6–7].

Christ had to touch the blind man, and the blind man had to obey Christ. Christ must touch our spiritual vision and bring new life to the dead spiritual optic nerve. It is not a question of who sinned. "For all have sinned, and come short of the glory of God" (Rom. 3:23). If Christ has not touched your eyes, you are not seeing.

There are so many people right in our churches today who are blind and don't know it. People write to me and say they listened to our Bible-teaching program for months; then all of a sudden their eyes were opened and they saw. Like the poor young man in the mine explosion, there are people standing in the light of the Word of God who say, "Why doesn't someone turn on the light?" That is exactly what Pontius Pilate did. He asked, "What is truth?" (John 18:38) as he was standing right in the presence of the One who said, "I am the way, the truth, and the life" (John 14:6). We need to let Christ touch our eyes so that we can see.

You will notice that Christ touched this man although the man still could not see Him. Then Jesus asked him to go wash, and the man obeyed. We may ask why Jesus used this method to heal the man. I think there are several reasons: (1) This Gospel sets forth the deity of Christ, but it also sets forth Jesus as a man. Jesus had just claimed His deity and now He touches the blind man, man to man. (2) The blind man must obey the Lord Jesus Christ if he is to see. (3) The Lord sent him to the pool which is called Siloam, and John makes a point of telling us *Siloam* means "Sent." Even the name of the pool bears testimony that Jesus is *sent* from the Father. Jesus may be implying to this man that He has been sent from the Father, and in the same way He is sending him. (4) The blind man needed the water to make him see. The water represents the Word of God in many passages of Scripture. It is my firm conviction that there never can be a conversion without the Word of God. "The entrance of thy words giveth light; it giveth understanding unto the simple" (Ps. 119:130). (5) The Jews needed this testimony because in verse 29 they say, "We know that God spake unto Moses: as for this fellow, we know not from whence he is." They must see by this healing of the blind man that Jesus is the God-man who is sent from the Father.

May I point out that the *method* of healing this man is not the important issue. The *Person* who heals is the important issue. It is Christ who opened his eyes. The blind man's part was to trust and obey.

Jesus used different methods of healing people. If the method was the touch, the man healed would insist everyone would need the same experience that he had. He would go away singing, "The Touch of His Hand on Mine." When Jesus healed others by not touching them at all, they would insist that one doesn't need to experience anything, not even His touch. They would say that all one needs is the Word of Jesus. They would go away singing, "Only Believe." Then, this blind man here would say to all of them that they are wrong. He'd say you've got to be touched and then you must go to the pool and wash; so he would be singing, "Shall We Gather at the River?" You are going to tell me that is perfectly absurd, silly, and ridiculous. It sure is, but I know a lot of "blind" folk today who will argue about the necessity of a certain ceremony or an experience to be saved. However, the all-important thing is to come to Christ, to believe Him, to obey Him. "Him that cometh to me I will in no wise cast out" (John 6:37). It is the person of the Lord Jesus Christ that is important.

I want to stop here and show how the condition of the blind man parallels our condition as sinners before we were saved.

1. The blind man was outside the temple, shut out from God. Remember that Paul says in Ephesians 2:12 that *we* were strangers from

the covenants of promise, that we had no hope; we were without God in the world. That is the condition of everyone before he is saved. Without God, without hope, shut out!

2. The man was blind. He was unable to see the Savior. John Hancock heard a sermon of John Witherspoon on the text, "I am the door: by me if any man enter in, he shall be saved" (John 10:9). As he walked home he thought to himself, "I have always admired John Witherspoon but tonight I didn't follow him. He impresses me as being a great preacher, but tonight I couldn't understand him." When he got home he put the key in the lock and pushed open the big door of his colonial home. He said, "Oh, I *see!*" His family laughed and said, "Of course, you see. You were out in the dark and now you have come into the light." He answered, "Yes, but I mean that I now see that Jesus is the door, and faith is the key that turns the lock. I now trust Christ, and I see Him."

We were blind without Christ. Did you see Him as your Savior before you were saved? Was He the wonderful One to you then? No. We were blind.

3. The man had been blind from birth. We were born in sin. We came into this world as sinners.

4. The blind man was beyond human help. Nobody had a cure for his blindness. We were helpless sinners in this world and no one had a cure for us.

5. He was a beggar. This is what hurts a lot of people. They hate to admit they are beggars. They would be willing to pay for salvation, but it is not for sale. You have to come to God for salvation as this beggar did. God *gives* it away. This beggar could never have bought salvation because he had nothing with which to buy it. "Ho, every one that thirsteth, come ye to the waters, and he that hath no money; come ye, buy, and eat; yea, come, buy wine and milk without money and without price" (Isa. 55:1).

6. He made no appeal to Jesus. Blind Bartimaeus was loud and insistent, but this man just sat there. He didn't know Jesus. It took him a long time to grow in grace and in the knowledge of Jesus Christ. Friend, did you really want to get saved? Were you looking for salvation? Were you looking for the Lord Jesus? If you are the average per-

son, you were not. You were not looking for Him, but He was looking for you. That is the story of man and his salvation.

7. There was no pity shown to him by others. The Jews passed him by on their way to the temple. The disciples wanted to argue about him. They had no intention of showing any mercy to this man, and they were not prepared to do anything for him. This is a picture of the human family. Christ feels compassion for us, and Christ alone can help us.

REACTION TO THE MIRACLE

There is a change in a man who had been blind. He no longer must feel his way home every day but walks home *seeing*. I think this man was shouting, "Hallelujah, I can see!"

1. The neighbors—

The neighbours therefore, and they which before had seen him that he was blind, said, Is not this he that sat and begged?

Some said, This is he: others said, He is like him: but he said, I am he [John 9:8–9].

Can't you picture the neighborhood? Someone stands at the window and says, "Look, there's the blind man." His wife goes to the door to look and says, "That's not the blind man. He looks like the blind man but he's not blind." So the man must identify himself to his own neighbors.

The neighbors knew something had happened to him. I do not believe that if you are truly converted, if you have changed from blindness to seeing, you can go on without people noticing that you have changed. If there is no evidence of a change, then something is wrong, radically wrong.

Therefore said they unto him, How were thine eyes opened?

> He answered and said, A man that is called Jesus made clay, and anointed mine eyes, and said unto me, Go to the pool of Siloam, and wash: and I went and washed, and I received sight.
>
> Then said they unto him, Where is he? He said, I know not [John 9:10-12].

I love the testimony of this man. He told only what he knew—a good, honest, sincere testimony. He grew in perception every time he gave his testimony. Notice how accurate the Word of God is. He didn't say Jesus took spittle and made clay. In his blindness he didn't know that. All he knew was that he felt clay rubbed on his eyes. His testimony is honest, not elaborated or glamorized.

Salvation is really a simple matter. It is coming to the Lord Jesus and experiencing the power of God. This man hadn't even seen Jesus and yet the Lord Jesus had opened his eyes. The important thing for us is not to see Jesus but to believe in Him.

2. The Pharisees—

> They brought to the Pharisees him that aforetime was blind.
>
> And it was the sabbath day when Jesus made the clay, and opened his eyes.
>
> Then again the Pharisees also asked him how he had received his sight. He said unto them, He put clay upon mine eyes, and I washed, and do see [John 9:13-15].

Again, the man's testimony is very simple. You would think these Pharisees would have rejoiced that a blind man could now see. You'd think they would break out in a "Hallelujah Chorus." Not this cold-blooded crowd! Now notice the reaction of the Pharisees. They just don't know what to do about a man born blind who is now walking around seeing.

Therefore said some of the Pharisees, This man is not of God, because he keepeth not the sabbath day. Others said, How can a man that is a sinner do such miracles? And there was a division among them [John 9:16].

These men were undoubtedly some of the cleverest men on earth. I believe beyond a shadow of a doubt that they would have been more than a match for the Greek philosophers. They were experts at arguing. They are going to use a syllogistic method of arguing. They have a major premise, a minor premise, and then a conclusion. If both the premises are true, the conclusion will be true. But if either of the premises is false, the conclusion will be false. Here is their reasoning:

Major premise—all people from God keep the Sabbath.

Minor premise—Jesus does not keep the Sabbath.

Conclusion—Jesus is not from God.

Their false major premise kept people from coming to the true conclusion. If both premises had been true, their conclusion would have been true.

Major premise—Only people from God can open the eyes of a man born blind.

Minor premise—Jesus opened the eyes of the blind man.

Conclusion—Jesus is from God.

Unfortunately, we find similar controversies going on in our churches today. There are arguments over nonessentials while the world outside is dying and going to hell, blind to the gospel. There is still the same old argument. "He doesn't keep the Sabbath"—which means "He doesn't do it our way."

They say unto the blind man again, What sayest thou of him, that he hath opened thine eyes? He said, He is a prophet.

But the Jews did not believe concerning him, that he had been blind, and received his sight, until they called the parents of him that had received his sight [John 9:17–18].

In their argumentation they ask, "How can a man that is a sinner do such miracles?" This is the very thing which helped the blind man to grow in his perception. If a sinner can't do such miracles, yet because of Him he can see, then this One must be a *prophet!* He must be from God. The blind man has taken another step.

"But the Jews did not believe concerning him." When men don't want to believe a thing, it is amazing what little peccadilloes they will attempt to dig up to really get away from the truth. Because they won't accept the man's testimony, they call in his parents.

3. The parents—

And they asked them, saying, Is this your son, who ye say was born blind? how then doth he now see?

His parents answered them and said, We know that this is our son, and that he was born blind:

But by what means he now seeth, we know not; or who hath opened his eyes, we know not: he is of age; ask him: he shall speak for himself.

These words spake his parents, because they feared the Jews: for the Jews had agreed already, that if any man did confess that he was Christ, he should be put out of the synagogue [John 9:19–22].

Here is religious conniving, and it is one of the most pernicious things that is imaginable. The religious rulers are trying to find somebody they can hang this on, and the parents want to get off the hook. These rulers never contested the fact that the man had been blind and now could see. It's only professors in swivel chairs in universities who doubt the miracles Jesus performed. The people who were present never denied that a miracle had been performed.

Therefore said his parents, He is of age; ask him [John 9:23].

The parents knew that a miracle had been done. But they were not prepared to explain *how* the miracle had been done. They did not want to be excommunicated because that would completely ostracize them, and they didn't want to get into that kind of trouble. Since the religious rulers cannot deny the miracle, they will try to keep the Lord Jesus from receiving the credit for it.

> **Then again called they the man that was blind, and said unto him, Give God the praise: we know that this man is a sinner [John 9:24].**

The Jews now go back to their first argument: this Man is a sinner because He broke the Sabbath. Don't give glory to this Man, the Lord Jesus. Give the glory to God. My, doesn't that sound nice and pious!

> **He answered and said, Whether he be a sinner or no, I know not: one thing I know, that, whereas I was blind, now I see [John 9:25].**

He hasn't seen the Lord Jesus yet. This is the second time they have brought him into court, and he is a little weary of the whole thing. Yet, listen to his testimony. "One thing I know, that, whereas I was blind, now I see."

That is the testimony of any sinner who has been saved. Once I was blind but now I see. Once I was in spiritual darkness but now I am in spiritual light. Once I did not know Christ, but now I know Him as my Savior. I don't know about you, but I get a little weary of long-winded testimonies. I suspect that many of them are padded and embellished and polished up to make them attractive. Sometimes the emphasis is placed on the past, so much so that the people actually come out as heroes in their testimony. They were leaders in crime, they were rubbing shoulders with the gang leaders, they knew all the great ones, they were the worst alcoholics, the worst gamblers, and on and on. Then they heard the gospel and were converted. The people who hear such testimonies go home and call their friends, "My, have you heard the testimony of So-and-So?"—and they are so busy telling about So-and-So and all the things he had done that they hardly even mention Christ. Friend, the important part of any testimony that I want to hear is simply this, "Once I was blind; now I see."

Then said they to him again, What did he to thee? how opened he thine eyes? [John 9:26].

The Pharisees are really up against it. They're trying their best to find some little flaw that they can seize upon to explain away the miracle that has been performed. They cannot simply dismiss it as theologians and professors try to do today. The man is there, and he can see.

He answered them, I have told you already, and ye did not hear: wherefore would ye hear it again? will ye also be his disciples?

Then they reviled him, and said, Thou art his disciple; but we are Moses' disciples [John 9:27–28].

The man who had been blind is beginning to understand what they are doing, and he gets a little sarcastic with them, "Will you also be His disciples?" He makes another interesting observation, "Will you hear it again?" Not only are the Pharisees blind so they cannot see the Light of the World, they are also deaf so they cannot hear.

We know that God spake unto Moses: as for this fellow, we know not from whence he is.

The man answered and said unto them, Why herein is a marvellous thing, that ye know not from whence he is, and yet he hath opened mine eyes.

Now we know that God heareth not sinners: but if any man be a worshipper of God, and doeth his will, him he heareth.

Since the world began was it not heard that any man opened the eyes of one that was born blind.

If this man were not of God, he could do nothing.

They answered and said unto him, Thou wast altogether born in sins, and dost thou teach us? And they cast him out [John 9:29–34].

The religious rulers revile him. You can notice again that, when men do not have an answer, they will resort to ridicule. Inadvertently they have slowly moved the healed blind man into a line of logic so that he knows only a man from God could do such a miracle: there is no doubt that he had been healed, so this Man must be from God. Remember, he still has never seen Jesus.

These rulers have no answer. They cannot meet the argument or give a satisfactory explanation. The facts confound and contradict them. What do they do? They cast the man out. This excommunication shut him out of the temple. It also shut him out of business. It made him an outcast, almost like a leper. He would be shut out of everything religious and social.

4. The blind man meets Jesus—

Jesus heard that they had cast him out; and when he had found him, he said unto him, Dost thou believe on the Son of God?

He answered and said, Who is he, Lord, that I might believe on him?

And Jesus said unto him, Thou hast both seen him, and it is he that talketh with thee.

And he said, Lord, I believe. And he worshipped him [John 9:35–38].

The Lord Jesus comes on the scene. This man has defended the Lord Jesus, has come out the winner in the argument, but has been cast out by the religious rulers. It is quite wonderful that the Lord Jesus comes to him. Friend, it is always Jesus who looks for the man. The Lord has prepared this man all along the way. Now the man must put his faith in the Son of God. Our Lord now comes to him with that crucial question: "Dost thou believe on the Son of God?" The experiences through which he has gone have strengthened his faith and clarified his thinking. The Lord knows that he is ready for this final step. This man is so very open, so honest and sincere. He asks who the Son of God is so that he might believe. You can see the eagerness of this man. He wants to go farther. He wants to come to know Him. Our Lord responds in this lovely way, "Thou hast both seen him, and it is he that talketh with thee." The man believes Him and worships Him. This is one of the finest instances of faith that we have in the entire Word of God. Our Lord took this blind man step by step and brought him to His feet where he could say, "Lord, I believe," and he worshiped Him.

It is so with the steps of every sinner. We are blind at first. We are lost sinners, and we don't even see our lost condition. Then we come to Christ. He reveals Himself to us; our eyes are opened and we see who He is and what He has done for us. Then the question is: "Will you believe?" This man's answer can also be your answer, "Lord, I believe." And you will fall at His feet and worship Him.

And Jesus said, For judgment I am come into this world, that they which see not might see; and that they which see might be made blind [John 9:39].

This seems to be a strange statement. The Lord says that there are those who have eyes and see not. They have physical eyes and physical sight, but they are blind spiritually. If a man will admit he is blind and will come to Jesus as a blind man, Jesus will give him spiritual insight. Paul writes: "But the natural man receiveth not the things of the Spirit of God: for they are foolishness unto him: neither can he know them, because they are spiritually discerned" (1 Cor. 2:14).

My friend, if you have come into the presence of the Lord Jesus, the Light of the World, and still say, "What is truth?" or, "I just don't see that He is my Savior," or, "I don't understand what this is about," then you are not seeing. You are spiritually blind. The Pharisees had eyes; they thought they saw; they were religious people, zealous people, and yet they were blind.

The heathen are lost. They are in darkness. Yet the Lord puts each man through a series of steps. If there is any man today out yonder in heathenism who wants to know about Jesus, the Lord will get the gospel to him. The man who sits in the church pew and hears the preaching of the Word of God and the giving out of the gospel is in the presence of the Light. That Light reveals his blindness. Jesus said, ". . . If therefore the light that is in thee be darkness, how great is that darkness!" (Matt. 6:23). If you know the facts about Jesus Christ, the Light of the World, but you will not believe, then, my friend, you are spiritually blind and there is nothing else to offer you. If you have been in the presence of the Savior of the world and have rejected Him, there is no other Savior to offer to you.

And some of the Pharisees which were with him heard these words, and said unto him, Are we blind also?

Jesus said unto them, If ye were blind, ye should have no sin: but now ye say, We see; therefore your sin remaineth [John 9:40–41].

We began with a blind man who was healed so that he saw, both physically and spiritually. We end with religious rulers who were terribly, tragically blind, yet who thought they could see. In the presence of Christ, in the presence of the Light, in the presence of the revelation of God, they said they had no sin.

Some of the most dogmatic people today are the atheists and the cultists. They say they see, but they are blind. They reject the Lord Jesus Christ, and so their sin remains. Although they are not walking around with a white walking stick, they are blind.

CHAPTER 10

*THEME: Jesus is the Good Shepherd (seventh word);
humanity—Christ in form of servant; deity—Christ
equal with God*

HUMANITY—CHRIST IN FORM OF SERVANT

The ancient sheepfold of that day still exists in many towns in that land. It was a public sheepfold. In the evening all the shepherds who lived in that town would bring their sheep to the sheepfold and turn them in for the night. They would entrust them to the porter who kept the sheep; then they would go to their homes for the night. The next morning the shepherds would identify themselves to the porter, and he would let them in the door to get their sheep.

1. "Door into the sheepfold"—

Verily, verily, I say unto you, He that entereth not by the door into the sheepfold, but climbeth up some other way, the same is a thief and a robber.

But he that entereth in by the door is the shepherd of the sheep [John 10:1–2].

The sheepfold represents the nation Israel. Jesus is telling them that He came in by the door. He goes on to say that anyone who doesn't come by the door, but climbs in some other way, is a thief and a robber. This is a tremendous claim that He is making here. He came in by the door. He came in legally. That is, He came in fulfillment of the prophecies of the Old Testament. He came in under the Law. "But when the fulness of the time was come, God sent forth his Son, made of a woman, made under the law" (Gal. 4:4). He came in the line of David according to prophecy (see Luke 1:32). He was born in Bethlehem according to prophecy (see Mic. 5:2). Not only was He in the line of David, but He was born of a virgin according to prophecy (see Isa.

7:14). At the time that He was born, He was a rod out of the stem of Jesse (see Isa. 11:1). Now this is interesting. By the time Jesus came, the royal line of David had dropped back to the level of the peasant. There was no royalty anymore. Jesse had been a farmer down in Bethlehem. In fact, he raised sheep. His son, David, had the anointing oil poured on him, and that line became the kingly line. But when the Lord Jesus was born, He was just a branch out of the stem of Jesse, the peasant. Jesus was simply a carpenter and wore a carpenter's robe. How accurately the prophecies were fulfilled!

He is the Messiah, and He came in through the door. No one else could have had the credentials that He had. Anyone else would have been a thief and a robber. They would not have had the credentials of the Messiah and would have had to climb over the fence. You see, in the preceding chapter, the man healed of his blindness had been excommunicated, put out of the temple. The religious rulers are rejecting the Lord Jesus, and now they are challenging Him. Remember they said, "Are we blind also?" Our Lord made it very clear that they were blind. Now He presents His credentials. This is a tremendous claim He is making in this chapter: Israel is the sheepfold; Jesus is the Good Shepherd.

To him the porter openeth; and the sheep hear his voice; and he calleth his own sheep by name, and leadeth them out [John 10:3].

Whom does the porter represent? The porter is the Holy Spirit. The Spirit of God came upon Jesus, and everything that He did, He did by the power of the Spirit of God. The Holy Spirit was opening the ears of His sheep to hear His voice. His sheep have responded. This ties in with the preceding chapter. Those religious rulers were blind spiritually and, what is more, they were deaf. They didn't even hear His voice. But He calls His own sheep by name and leads them out. The blind man heard Him call. Simon heard His call, and Jesus changed his name to Peter, which means a stone. He called James and John, Nathanael and Philip. He stopped under a tree in Jericho and called Zacchaeus. He calls His sheep by name.

Let me digress for a moment to say that when the Lord Jesus calls His own out of the world at the time of the Rapture, I believe that His call will have every believer's name in it. I think I'll hear Him say personally, "Vernon McGee." That will be wonderful! He knows my name, you see, and He'll call it at that time. And He'll call you if you are one of His sheep. You will hear your name in His shout!

He leads His sheep out of the sheepfold, out of Judaism. You see, the religious rulers had excommunicated the man whose sight Jesus had restored. Jesus is going to lead this sheep out of Judaism.

And when he putteth forth his own sheep, he goeth before them, and the sheep follow him: for they know his voice [John 10:4].

When I was near Bethlehem, I spent some time looking over a sheepfold that was still in use. A sheepfold is an enclosure where shepherds put their sheep for the night. The porter has charge of it. Then the shepherd spends the night in his own bed. When he comes to the sheepfold in the morning, his sheep are all mixed up with somebody else's sheep—there is no brand or marking on the sheep. How does he get the sheep that are his? He calls them by name. The sheep don't have to be identified; they know their shepherd's voice. When he starts out over the hill, his own sheep come out of the fold and follow him. They know him. Our Lord says, "The sheep will follow him because they know his voice."

It is the most wonderful thing in the world to know that, when we give out the Word of God, Jesus is calling His sheep. The Spirit of God is the Porter who does the opening, and the sheep will hear. Our Lord will lead His sheep out of a legal system, perhaps even out of a church where they're not being fed. They will follow Him. You cannot permanently fool God's sheep. It is true that the sheep may get into a cult or an "ism" for a while, but the sheep will recognize the voice of the Shepherd. Unfortunately, many preachers are afraid to stand up for the truth; however, when a man preaches the Word of God, the sheep will hear it. We can depend on that because our Lord said, "My sheep hear my voice" (v. 27).

And a stranger will they not follow, but will flee from him: for they know not the voice of strangers [John 10:5].

I believe that you can fool some of God's people some of the time, but I don't think you can fool God's people all the time. For a time, God's sheep may *think* they hear Him but eventually discover that it is not His voice. Then they will turn to the teaching of the Word of God because they know their Shepherd. It is amazing. I have been teaching the Word of God for about forty years and have learned again and again that when His sheep hear His voice, they will follow Him.

For a long time I worried about those who will not listen to the message. I have reached the point that I don't worry about them. The reason they don't hear His voice is that they are not His sheep. Wherever we find people who are eager for the Word of God, we know they are His sheep.

This parable spake Jesus unto them: but they understood not what things they were which he spake unto them [John 10:6].

The word *parable* is really not an accurate translation. The Greek word for parable is *parabolē* and the word in this verse is *paroimia*, which really means "an allegory." The Gospel of John does not record any of the parables of our Lord. It records the metaphors and allegories such as "I am the light of the world" (John 8:12) and "I am the bread of life" (John 6:35). These are not parables but are figures of speech to let us know something about God. They are intended to give us light on the subject so that we can see. So it should actually read, "This allegory spake Jesus unto them." They didn't understand what He was saying because, as He had said, they were blind.

Our Lord also said, "Who hath ears to hear, let him hear" (Matt. 13:9). It is possible to have ears and yet not hear. They hear it all right, but they don't hear it as the Word of God. That is the important thing. Beloved, how do you hear it? It is this important difference in hearing to which our Lord referred when He quoted Isaiah, ". . . By hearing ye shall hear, and shall not understand; and seeing ye shall see, and shall not perceive" (Matt. 13:14).

2. "Door of the sheep"—

Then said Jesus unto them again, Verily, verily, I say unto you, I am the door of the sheep.

All that ever came before me are thieves and robbers: but the sheep did not hear them [John 10:7–8].

Here He gives another allegory. He has spoken about the door of the sheepfold, but now He moves one more step and says that He is the *Door* of the sheep. The Lord Jesus is the Door for those coming out of Israel. They had just cast the blind man out of the synagogue, out of the sheepfold. Immediately the Lord Jesus had come to this man and revealed Himself to him. When the Lord revealed Himself to the man, He became the Door for this man. The man had been brought out of the sheepfold and to the Lord Jesus Christ to follow Him. This is the second great truth which our Lord is stating in this chapter.

Our Lord will state this same principle in John 15 when He says, "I am the true vine . . . ye are the branches" (John 15:1, 5). The vine in the Old Testament is a picture of the nation Israel. Jesus is saying that it is no longer the connection with the nation Israel but the relationship with Him which is the joining of the branches with the Vine. They must come out from Judaism, come out from ritualism, and come to Him. He is saying that He is the Door. Remember, He is talking to the religious rulers. By the way, some of them did come to Him after His resurrection.

3. "The Door"—

I am the door: by me if any man enter in, he shall be saved, and shall go in and out, and find pasture.

The thief cometh not, but for to steal, and to kill, and to destroy: I am come that they might have life, and that they might have it more abundantly [John 10:9–10].

Jesus Christ is the Way. He is the only Way. He is the Way *out* for you and He is the Way *in* for you. He has come to bring us an abundant life.

The thief comes to steal, to kill, and to destroy. I think this is a test you can apply to a church, a religious organization, a radio or television program. Is it a religious racket? Is somebody getting rich out of it? Compare it to the Good Shepherd who came to save sinners and to give us life, abundant life.

Here is a brief review of this passage:

1. "Door into the sheepfold" (v. 1). The sheepfold is the nation Israel. Jesus will lead His sheep out of Judaism, out from under a legalistic system.

2. "Door of the sheep" (v. 7). Jesus is the Door for those coming out of Judaism (e.g., the excommunicated man who had been blind); He has called them out. ". . . Save yourselves from this untoward generation" (Acts 2:40).

3. "The Door" (v. 9). Jesus Christ is the Door for both Jew and Gentile. He is the Door of salvation. Freedom to go in and out and find pasture is the liberty of the sons of God in Christ Jesus.

4. "The Good Shepherd"—

> **I am the good shepherd: the good shepherd giveth his life for the sheep.**
>
> **But he that is an hireling, and not the shepherd, whose own the sheep are not, seeth the wolf coming, and leaveth the sheep, and fleeth: and the wolf catcheth them, and scattereth the sheep.**
>
> **The hireling fleeth, because he is an hireling, and careth not for the sheep [John 10:11–13].**

How can Jesus be the Door and the Shepherd at the same time? Actually, there was no door that swung on hinges and had a padlock to secure the sheepfold. The man who was guarding it slept across the doorway so that he himself was the door. Jesus is not only the Door, but He is also the Good Shepherd, the One who stays in the doorway.

He is the Door which opens to eternal life; He is the One who protects His own; He is also the Good Shepherd.

Jesus is also called the Lamb of God. How can He be the Lamb of God and at the same time be the Good Shepherd? This may sound like mixed metaphors, but it is one of the most glorious truths in Scripture. He is the "Lamb of God, which taketh away the sin of the world" (John 1:29). He came down and identified Himself with us who are the sheep—but He is the Shepherd also. The fact that He became a Lamb emphasizes the humanity of Jesus Christ. The fact that He is the Good Shepherd emphasizes the deity of Christ. He alone was worthy and able to save us. No other human being could do this; He had to be God.

The Lord Jesus Christ has a threefold relationship to this flock which is known as His church. First of all He is the *Good Shepherd*, and He defines the Good Shepherd in verse 11: "I am the good shepherd: the good shepherd giveth his life for the sheep." Then He is the *Great Shepherd*, for we read in the magnificent benediction given in Hebrews 13:20: "Now the God of peace, who brought again from the dead the great shepherd of the sheep with the blood of an eternal covenant, even our Lord Jesus, make you perfect in every good thing to do his will . . ." (ASV). So today He is the Great Shepherd of the sheep, as seen in Psalm 23. But wait, that does not give the total picture. He is also the *Chief Shepherd*. This speaks of the future. Peter says in his first epistle, "And when the chief Shepherd shall appear, ye shall receive a crown of glory that fadeth not away" (1 Pet. 5:4).

The hireling does not care for the sheep. Founders of some of the world religions did very little for their followers. Modern cult leaders actually get rich off the people. In contrast to this, the Good Shepherd gives His life for the sheep, and He protects His own.

I am the good shepherd, and know my sheep, and am known of mine.

As the Father knoweth me, even so know I the Father: and I lay down my life for the sheep [John 10:14–15].

Here is a wonderful relationship. He knows His sheep, and His sheep know Him. Paul wrote, "That I may know him, and the power of his resurrection . . ." (Phil. 3:10). To know Him is to love Him. In this connection one should read what God says about shepherds in His message through Ezekiel, chapter 34.

Notice that this is the third time that He says His sheep know Him. To know Jesus Christ is all-important, and everything else becomes secondary. That is one reason I have given up arguing about nonessentials. Let's stop arguing about religion and about details. The important issue is to know Jesus Christ. Do you hear His voice; do you know the Shepherd?

There is no shepherd like this One. David risked his life to save his sheep from a bear and from a lion. The Son of David gave His life for His sheep.

> **And other sheep I have, which are not of this fold: them also I must bring, and they shall hear my voice; and there shall be one fold, and one shepherd [John 10:16].**

There are other sheep which are not of this fold—the fold is Israel—but others will also hear His voice, and there shall be one flock and one Shepherd. It is really "flock" (poimnē), not "fold" (aulē), in this second phrase. You see, there is to be one flock and one Shepherd. There is to be the one flock containing Jew and Gentile, rich and poor, bond and free, male and female, black and white, people from every nation and out of every tongue and tribe.

> **Therefore doth my Father love me, because I lay down my life, that I might take it again.**
>
> **No man taketh it from me, but I lay it down of myself. I have power to lay it down, and I have power to take it again. This commandment have I received of my Father [John 10:17–18].**

He says that all of this is the will of the Father. The Father loves Him because He died for us. We also ought to love Him because He died for us. He made His soul an offering for sin. On the cross during those three hours of darkness, God the Father put upon Him the sin of the world, and He went through hell for you and me. The Good Shepherd gave His life for the sheep.

He makes it very clear that He gave His life willingly. He was in full control at His trial. Also He set the time of His death. The Jews said it shouldn't be on a feast day lest there be an uproar, a riot of the people, but He *was* crucified on the feast day. He was never more kingly than when He went to the Cross. If one reads the Gospels carefully, one is aware that actually the Roman government was on trial, the nation Israel was on trial, you and I were on trial. Although He didn't have to die, He did it willingly for the sins of the world. "Looking unto Jesus the author and finisher of our faith; who for the joy that was set before him endured the cross, despising the shame . . ." (Heb. 12:2). No man could take His life from Him. He claimed power to lay down His life and to take it again.

There was a division therefore again among the Jews for these sayings.

And many of them said, He hath a devil, and is mad; why hear ye him?

Others said, These are not the words of him that hath a devil. Can a devil open the eyes of the blind? [John 10:19–21].

This refers to the fact that He opened the eyes of the man who was born blind. The crowd there that day said, "Well, a demon could never have done what He did!" There is a division. Why? Because some are sheep and some are not. Sheep will hear and the others will not hear.

The issue is still the same today as it was then. Either the Lord Jesus Christ was a madman or He is the Savior of the world. Either He has a demon or He is the Son of God. There has always been that division. When Paul preached at Athens, some believed and some did not.

When I preach, some believe and some do not. We cannot expect it to be any different.

The so-called liberal theologians are the most inconsistent and illogical people. Jesus Christ cannot be only a good teacher and a great example. He is either a fraud or He is the Son of God. Jesus Christ puts you on the horns of a dilemma, my friend. He is a madman or He is your God and your Savior.

DEITY—CHRIST EQUAL WITH GOD

And it was at Jerusalem the feast of the dedication, and it was winter [John 10:22].

The Feast of Tabernacles was in the last part of October; the Feast of Dedication was in the last part of December—so there was a two-month interval. This feast celebrated the time when Judas Maccabaeus delivered the temple from Antiochus Ephiphanes, the Syrian, who had polluted it. This took place in 167 B.C. and was still celebrated in our Lord's day.

"And it was winter." Jesus is through with the nation. From here on, in the Gospel of John, He talks to His own. He will not make another public call. It is now too late for the harvest. The Lamb of God is being shut up in preparation to go to the Cross and die for the sins of the world.

Friend, may I remind you that you can play at this thing too long. Winter is coming for you. There will come a day when you won't be able to witness. If you are going to do anything for Him, you had better do it now. If you have never sincerely accepted Jesus Christ as your Savior, may I remind you that winter can come for that, too. There does come a time when it is too late, my beloved, too late to be saved. You can persist in rejecting the Lord Jesus Christ so long that finally you will be unable to accept Him. The prophet spoke of this eventuality: "The harvest is past, the summer is ended, and we are not saved" (Jer. 8:20).

And Jesus walked in the temple in Solomon's porch.

Then came the Jews round about him, and said unto him, How long dost thou make us to doubt? If thou be the Christ, tell us plainly [John 10:23–24].

There was a big porch out there which was for the Gentiles, for those who were outside the nation Israel. Our Lord was no longer coming into the temple. It was winter, and He walked in Solomon's porch.

Jesus had made His identity very clear, and those who accepted Him understood that He was the Messiah, the Christ. Remember that Andrew had told his brother, "We have found the Messiah (see John 1:41). Nathanael recognized Him, "Rabbi, thou art the Son of God; thou art the King of Israel" (John 1:49). The Samaritan woman understood who He was; and the Samaritan men said, "Now we believe, not because of thy saying: for we have heard him ourselves, and know that this is indeed the Christ, the Saviour of the world" (John 4:42). Also the man healed of his blindness believed and worshiped Him. Now these religious leaders with their subtle questions are actually casting the blame on Him! They make it sound as if it is Jesus' fault for not giving enough information, whereas it is their lack of will to believe what God had revealed to them. Well, Jesus has revealed His messiahship to those who will hear, and now He declares it to these religious rulers.

Jesus answered them, I told you, and ye believed not: the works that I do in my Father's name, they bear witness of me.

But ye believe not, because ye are not of my sheep, as I said unto you [John 10:25–26].

Jesus tells them that He has the proofs of His messiahship. His works bear witness to it. He was born in the line of David, according to prophecy. He was introduced by John the Baptist. No man taught as He taught. No man could convict Him of sin. When John the Baptist sent his disciples to find out whether Jesus was the Messiah or whether they should look for another, Jesus told them to go back and tell John the Baptist the things that He was doing. Then John the Baptist would know the He had the credentials of the Messiah. You see, His teaching demonstrated that He was the Messiah, His life demonstrated it, and His miracles demonstrated it. The problem was not in His lack of credentials. The problem was in the unbelieving heart. The fact that they did not believe demonstrated that they were not His sheep. That's the negative side. Now He states the positive side.

> **My sheep hear my voice, and I know them, and they follow me:**
>
> **And I give unto them eternal life; and they shall never perish, neither shall any man pluck them out of my hand.**
>
> **My Father, which gave them me, is greater than all; and no man is able to pluck them out of my Father's hand.**
>
> **I and my Father are one [John 10:27–30].**

His sheep hear His voice. And they follow Him. The brand of ownership on the sheep is obedience. Do you want to know whether a person is saved or not? Then see if he is obeying Christ. Our ears must be open to His voice. "The hearing ear, and the seeing eye, the LORD hath made even both of them" (Prov. 20:12).

"I know them." I'm glad somebody knows me, aren't you? I am sometimes misunderstood, and I have to explain myself to people. However, I never need to explain anything to Him. He knows when I'm putting up an excuse; He knows when I am evading an issue; He understands me. He knows.

"And they follow me." I believe in the eternal security of the believer and in the insecurity of the make-believer. "They follow me"— it's just that simple. If the shepherd called his sheep one morning and started up the hill, and out of five hundred sheep in the sheepfold, one hundred came out and followed him, then I would conclude that those one hundred were his sheep. And I would also conclude that the other four hundred were not his sheep.

"And I give unto them eternal life; and they shall never perish." Friend, when He gives to them eternal life, that means they don't earn it and they don't work for it. He *gives* it to them. Note that it is *eternal* life. It is forever. If it plays out in a week or in a year or until they sin, then it is not eternal life after all. They are not really His sheep if the life does not last forever. The sheep may be in danger, but the Shepherd will protect them. They may be scattered, but He will gather them up again. They shall never perish.

May they backslide? Yes. Will they perish? No. The sheep may get into a pigpen, but there has never yet been a sheep in a pigpen that stayed in a pigpen. Sheep and pigs do not live together. The sheep is always a sheep. No man can pluck that sheep out of the Savior's hand. No enemy, no man, no created being can pluck them out of His hand. This is wonderful! One time a fellow gave me the argument that one can jump out of His hand because we are free moral agents. Listen to the passage. It actually says "no created thing shall pluck them out of my hand." He is the Shepherd. He is God. If you think you can jump out, the Father puts His hand right down on you, and you can't do any jumping. Brother, He's got you and you can't get loose. Both hands are the hands of Deity. No created thing can take the sheep out of His hand.

Years ago a Texas rancher told me about sheep. He said he had two thousand sheep, and someone had to be watching them all the time. If two little sheep go over the hill and get half a mile from the flock, they are lost. They cannot find their way back by themselves. The only way in the world they can be safe is for the shepherd to be there. If a wolf would come up and eat one of the little sheep, you'd think the other one would be smart enough to say, "He ate my little brother, so I'll go back over the hill and join the flock." No, he doesn't know where to go. All he does is go, "Baa," and run around and wait to be dessert for the wolf. A sheep is stupid. Neither has a sheep any way to defend himself. A sheep can't even outrun his enemy. If a sheep is safe, it is not because the sheep is clever or smart. It is because he has a good shepherd.

When I say to you that He gives me eternal life and I shall never perish, you may accuse me of bragging. No, my friend, I am not bragging on myself; I'm bragging about my Shepherd. I have a wonderful Shepherd. He won't lose any of His sheep. If He starts with one hundred, He will not end with ninety-nine. If one gets lost, He will go out and find it. None will be lost.

Then He says that He and the Father are one. He claims to be God.

Then the Jews took up stones again to stone him.

Jesus answered them, Many good works have I shewed you from my Father; for which of those works do ye stone me?

The Jews answered him, saying, For a good work we stone thee not; but for blasphemy; and because that thou, being a man, makest thyself God [John 10:31–33].

There is one thing that is sure: in that day, those who heard Him understood that He made Himself God. He produced His credentials. There was no way they could deny His miracles. He healed people by the thousands, and there was no denying the evidence. They accused Him of blasphemy. They accused Him of calling Himself God. And do you know, that is exactly what He was doing!

Jesus answered them, Is it not written in your law, I said, Ye are gods?

If he called them gods, unto whom the word of God came, and the scripture cannot be broken;

Say ye of him, whom the Father hath sanctified, and sent into the world, Thou blasphemest; because I said, I am the Son of God?

If I do not the works of my Father, believe me not.

But if I do, though ye believe not me, believe the works: that ye may know, and believe, that the Father is in me, and I in him [John 10:34–38].

Their accusation was that He as a man makes Himself God. He quotes to them Psalm 82:6, "I have said, Ye are gods; and all of you are children of the most High." Men are called to be the children of God, but Jesus is unique because He is the Man "whom the Father hath sanctified." He is the One who has been set apart. He is different from any other man in the world. He has been sent on a mission to the world. He is in the Father and the Father is in Him.

Therefore they sought again to take him: but he escaped out of their hand,

And went away again beyond Jordan into the place where John at first baptized; and there he abode.

And many resorted unto him, and said, John did no miracle: but all things that John spake of this man were true.

And many believed on him there [John 10:39–42].

John the Baptist did no miracles, but he bore a true testimony to the Messiah. Jesus is the Messiah, the Christ. He is the One who was to come. What think ye of Christ? This is the way to test your position. You can't be right in any of the rest unless you are first right in your thinking about Him. What think ye of Christ? If you are His sheep, you will hear His voice. If you are not, you will not hear Him. His voice will be drowned out in the babble of voices speaking to you. His sheep are able to hear the Son of God.

BIBLIOGRAPHY
(Recommended for Further Study)

Gaebelein, Arno C. *The Gospel of John*. Neptune, New Jersey: Loizeaux Brothers, 1925. (Fine exposition.)

Harrison, Everett F. *John: The Gospel of Faith*. Chicago, Illinois: Moody Press, 1962. (A survey.)

Hendriksen, William. *Gospel of John*. Grand Rapids, Michigan: Baker Book House, 1954.

Ironside, H. A. *Addresses on the Gospel of John*. Neptune, New Jersey: Loizeaux Brothers, 1942.

Kelly, William. *An Exposition of the Gospel of John*. Oak Park, Illinois: Bible Truth Publishers, 1898.

Kent, Homer A., Jr. *Fight in the Darkness: Studies in the Gospel of John*. Grand Rapids, Michigan: Baker Book House, 1975. (Excellent for personal or group study.)

Meyer, F. B. *The Gospel of John*. Fort Washington, Pennsylvania: Christian Literature Crusade, n.d. (Devotional.)

Morgan, G. Campbell. *The Gospel According to John*. Old Tappan, New Jersey: Fleming H. Revell Company, n.d.

Pentecost, J. Dwight. *The Parables of Our Lord*. Grand Rapids, Michigan: Zondervan Publishing House, 1982.

Pentecost, J. Dwight. *The Words and Works of Jesus Christ*. Grand Rapids, Michigan: Zondervan Publishing House, 1981.

Pink, Arthur W. *The Gospel of John*. Grand Rapids, Michigan: Zondervan Publishing House, 1945. (Comprehensive.)

Robertson, A. T. *Epochs in the Life of the Apostle John*. Grand Rapids, Michigan: Baker Book House, 1935.

Ryle, J. C. *Expository Thoughts on the Gospels.* 4 vols. Grand Rapids, Michigan: Baker Book House, n.d.

Scroggie, W. Graham. *The Gospel of John.* Grand Rapids, Michigan: Zondervan Publishing House, n.d. (Good outlines.)

Tenney, Merrill C. *John: The Gospel of Belief.* Grand Rapids, Michigan: Wm. B. Eerdmans Publishing Co., 1948.

Van Ryn, August. *Meditations in John.* Neptune, New Jersey: Loizeaux Brothers, n.d.

Vine, W. E. *John: His Record of Christ.* Grand Rapids, Michigan: Zondervan Publishing House, 1948.

Vos, Howard F. *Beginnings in the Life of Christ.* Chicago, Illinois: Moody Press, 1975. (Excellent, inexpensive survey.)